Early Learning Ski

Early Learning Skills Analysis

Mel Ainscow
Tutor (Special Education Needs) Cambridge Institute of Education

David A. Tweddle
General Advisor (Special Needs, Oldham)

David Fulton Publishers
London

Reprinted October 1986
April 1988
August 1989
February 1995

British Library Cataloguing in Publication Data:

Ainscow, Mel
Early learning skills analysis.
1. Primary schools. Students. Learning skills. Assessment – for teaching
I. Title II. Tweddle. David A.
372.12′64

ISBN 1 85346 027 3

Printed and bound in Great Britain.

Contents

Preface

The aim of this book is to help teachers in primary schools provide appropriate curriculum and teaching for pupils with special educational needs. It contains a procedure known as ELSA (i.e. Early Learning Skills Analysis), which is based on current ideas with regard to curriculum planning and assessment for such pupils, and stresses the importance of the class teacher's structured observation as the main assessment technique.

The book has been written in response to recent changes in thinking about the ways in which children's special needs should be met. In particular it is now recognized that a much larger proportion of children have learning difficulties at some point in their school careers. The bulk of these youngsters are, of course, in ordinary schools and it seems inevitable that they will be joined increasingly by children with more serious handicaps.

Recent legislation in a number of countries places teachers in ordinary schools in a position where they will be expected to take more specific responsibility for the education of pupils with special needs. In this country, for example, the 1981 Education Act necessitates all schools having appropriate procedures for the identification, assessment, and support of these pupils. In the United States Public Law 94–142 requires that children with special needs should be provided with an individualized education programme. ELSA provides a range of procedures which will help schools and individual teachers as they respond to these new demands.

Whilst our main purpose is to provide direct help to primary school teachers, the materials and ideas presented in this book should be relevant to others involved in remedial and special education. Members of the various advisory and support services (e.g. remedial specialists and educational psychologists) will find ELSA useful when setting up appropriate support programmes for individual pupils. Teachers in special classes, units, or schools may also wish to use the materials as a basis for developing a 'core' curriculum of basic skills.

Whatever the setting ELSA helps teachers to assess pupil progress within the curriculum and devise individual teaching programmes related to precise areas of need. We must stress that such programmes are seen as being in addition to the normal school activities that all children should experience. This is extremely important since we do not wish to encourage situations in which youngsters with special needs are separated from the opportunities provided for their classmates.

In addition to the design of teaching programmes the book also includes detailed procedures for recording pupil progress. Such records are important if teachers are to help children with learning difficulties succeed and, indeed, will be necessary where legislation requires pupil progress to be monitored and reviewed on a regular basis. This will be the case where a child is subject to a 'statement' as a result of the 1981 Education Act.

We want readers to take particular note of the emphasis placed on flexibility. The programmes and materials presented do not pretend to be a formal test or a complete curriculum. Rather they are a means of helping teachers assess and monitor the progress of individual children within the school's own curriculum. Consequently it will be necessary for the materials to be adapted and matched to the schemes operating within any particular school. With this in mind we have agreed with the publishers that Chapter 2, the assessment materials and the various record forms, may be reproduced for classroom use.

ELSA has been used and evaluated extensively, and has undergone considerable modifications over a period of five years. We would like to thank the many colleagues who have contributed to this work, especially the teachers who have tried the materials in their classrooms. In particular we are grateful to Jill Gardner and Jim Muncey, some of whose ideas have influenced the content of the text; Pat Kenward and Liz Mason for their work on the Alphabetical Spelling List; Stan Parry, the teacher involved in the parent project described in Chapter 8; Will Thompson who drew the illustrations in the assessment material; and Klaus Wedell, Sean Cameron, and Edgar Stones who read the draft of the book and made useful suggestions.

Finally we must thank May Chubb for her careful typing of this script and our families for their patience and support during the long gestation period of the book.

Mel Ainscow and David A. Tweddle
December 1982

Notes for Course Tutors

Much of the material in this book has been used within the context of in-service courses and workshops that we have conducted in various parts of the country during the past few years. It is presented and arranged here in a format which should facilitate its use as the basis for an introductory course on the use of objectives in planning teaching programmes. This may form part of training courses for teachers or educational psychologists, or could be a short course offered within the in-service programme of a local education authority.

Two possible delivery systems that might be adopted by tutors designing a course based on this book are:

1. *Lectures.* Here the main ideas would be presented in a series of formal presentations, perhaps illustrated by overhead projector slides or written notes, and supplemented by small group discussions and workshop activities.
2. *Workshops.* Each participant would be required to read the appropriate section of this book prior to attendance at the sessions. These would simply be discussions about the main ideas and practical assignments being carried out in the classroom between the sessions.

Whichever approach is adopted we suggest that at least five one-hour sessions at weekly intervals are required to cover the content of Chapters 1 to 6.

Each chapter begins with a goal (or goals) which should be used to guide the learning which is to take place within a course session. At the end of Chapters 3 to 6 there are some features which course tutors may find useful. They are:

1. *Self-tests.* These are intended to provide an informal method by which students can evaluate their own learning. Within the context of a course they might be used in a light-hearted way at the end of each session. This would also provide a useful summary of the main points covered.
2. *Discussion points.* Where there is time for group activities to supplement formal lectures these suggestions might be given to group leaders as a means of structuring discussion. In the main they attempt to focus on the practical implications of the ideas presented in the chapter.
3. *Classroom assignments.* Since it is important to relate theoretical principles to classroom situations during in-service training, we recommend that participants should carry out the practical assignments with at least one child.

If time is available a course might usefully be extended to allow participants the opportunity to carry out group assignments using the daily measurement and task analysis procedures described in Chapter 7. Experience has shown that this type of activity is a very potent form of in-service training, not least of which in making teachers more aware of the need to plan and implement teaching programmes systematically.

ACKNOWLEDGEMENT

The extract on page 184 is taken from the *Key Words Reading Scheme* by William Murrary, published by Ladybird Books, and is printed with the permission of the publishers.

1

Introducing ELSA

Chapter Goal
To describe the contents and function of ELSA

It is now widely accepted that special education should not be the preserve of children in special schools. About twenty per cent. of children need special educational help of one kind or another at some stage of their school life, but only one or two per cent. should need to attend special school. In other words, the vast majority of children who need special education should receive it in the normal classroom.

Most experienced teachers would say that this is all well and good in theory, but in practice there are two outstanding problems:

1. How are teachers in ordinary schools supposed to keep up to date with the research and specialized teaching techniques associated with special education? And
2. How are they intended to find the time to incorporate these techniques into their work with classes of thirty pupils or more?

The aim of this book is to help class teachers provide special education in the primary school classroom. It assumes neither advanced training nor practical experience in special education. It uses extensively researched teaching strategies but reduces technical jargon to a minimum. Most important, it is designed to be used by the teacher who has thirty or more pupils in the classroom.

This approach to teaching children with learning difficulties is described in the authors' book *Preventing Classroom Failure: An Objectives Approach* published by Wiley in 1979. The procedures and materials presented here represent an extension of the work described in that book, and have been developed over a period of several years of classroom trials.

What is ELSA?

ELSA stands for Early Learning Skills Analysis. The materials consist of one hundred and twenty-two carefully selected and precisely stated teaching objectives in arithmetic, handwriting, independence (or self-help) skills, language, motor skills, reading, and spelling. Experience has shown that the range of skills covered by these objectives is most suitable for children in nursery and infant classes and perhaps the first year of junior school. Teachers in special schools or units may also find them useful with older pupils.

ELSA can be used for

1. *Finding out what a pupil can and cannot do.* Assessment should be concerned primarily with determining precisely what each pupil can and cannot do. Moreover, it should be carried out in the classroom by the class teacher. ELSA provides a means of carrying out such an assessment using the placement test which is described in Chapter 3.
2. *Deciding what to teach.* Young children experiencing difficulties in learning must be set work at exactly the right level — not too easy and not too difficult. This decision can only be made on the basis of a detailed knowledge of what each pupil can and cannot do. Chapter 4 describes how to use placement test results to decide which skills to teach and what order to teach them.
3. *Planning teaching strategies.* ELSA does not restrict the teacher's choice of teaching methods and materials, but it does provide a rational basis for making such decisions. Chapter 5 describes how this can be achieved and looks at the implications of ELSA for issues like classroom organization, the systematic use of praise and reward, and the effective involvement of parents and classroom assistants.
4. *Keeping accurate records of pupil progress.* Assessment today is seen as a continuous classroom process concerned with monitoring pupils' progress. The teacher should be able to describe accurately — and at any time — what the pupil can already do, when he learnt to do it, what he is currently working on, when he started work on it, and how good he is expected to get at it. Chapter 6 describes how ELSA helps the teacher to do all of this quickly and easily.

These four main uses of ELSA are illustrated in Figure 1. The direction of the arrows indicates a logical sequence of decisions to be made by the teacher. The significance of the feedback arrow should be obvious. If you keep detailed records of the kind described here you will always know what the pupil can and cannot do. You can therefore decide what to teach next without doing another placement test.

Chapters 3 to 6 deal with these four main uses in sequence and explain in detail how ELSA can be used to make decisions at each stage. We would recommend, therefore, that Chapters 3 to 6 are read in sequence.

Chapter 7 deals with two advanced techniques, task analysis and daily measurement, which can, where appropriate, be incorporated into your use of ELSA. These should be particularly relevant in situations such as special schools or units where children can be given a greater amount of individual attention. Finally, Chapter 8 consists of six accounts of the application of ELSA in a variety of contexts, indicating particularly the importance of using it in a flexible manner.

A summary of the important points appears at the end of Chapters 3 to 6 in the form of a short test. This provides you with a check of your understanding of the ideas presented. We suggest that after reading a chapter you write the answers to each item on a scrap of paper and check them against the correct answers presented on the following page. When you make a mistake you

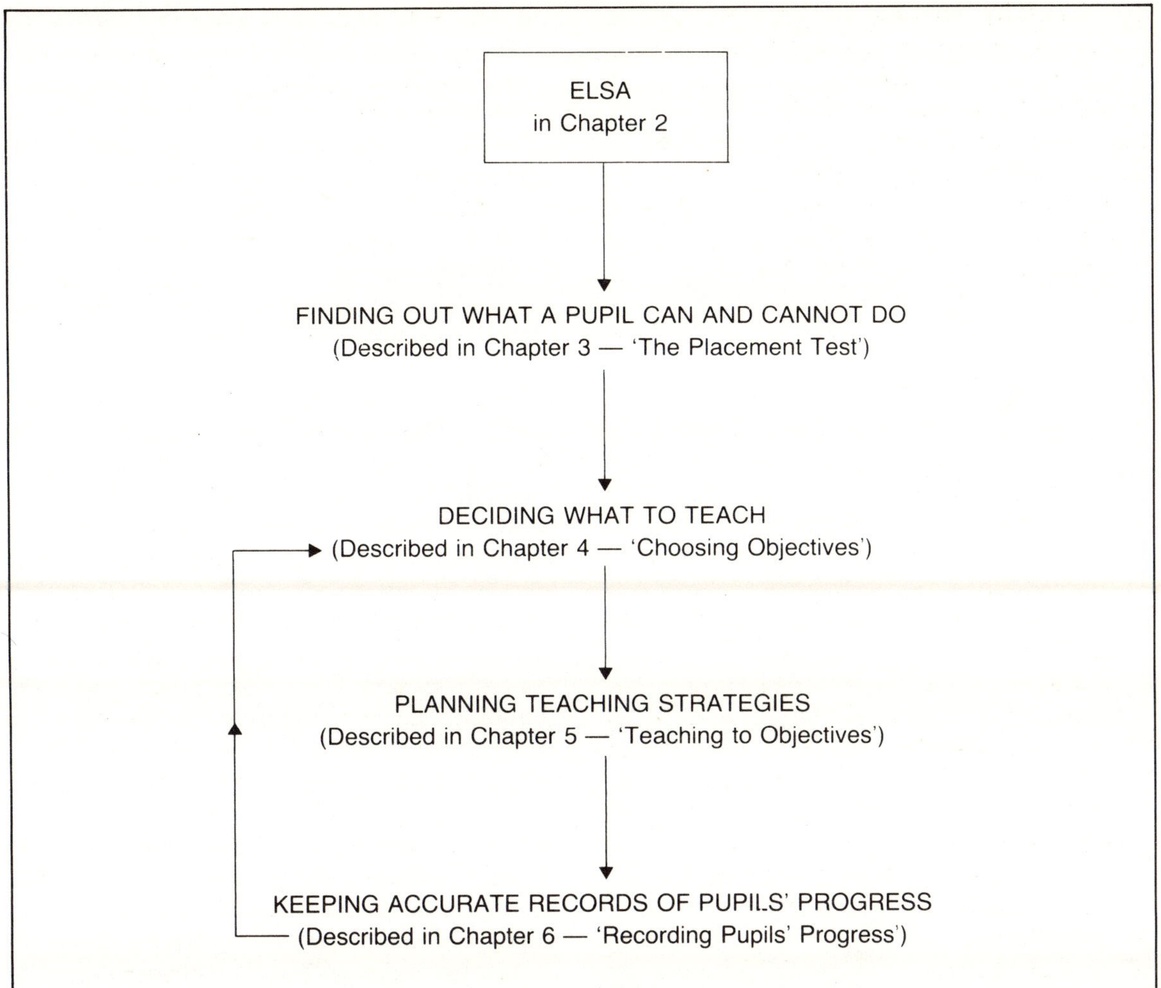

Figure 1: The four main uses of ELSA

should reread the appropriate section in the text, as indicated in brackets after each correct answer, before going on to read the next chapter.

The ELSA materials

Chapter 2 *is* ELSA. We would recommend strongly that you spend time perusing this material before proceeding to the explanations of its use in the classroom. You will find these subsequent chapters much easier to assimilate if you have studied the formats and conventions used in the material. The following notes will help you locate the various components of ELSA. The materials consist of subject areas, units, teaching objectives, pupil records, and assessment materials.

1. *Subject areas*

The areas covered by ELSA are: arithmetic, handwriting, independence skills, language, motor skills, reading, and spelling.

2. *Units*

The seven subject areas are each divided into between two and ten units. There is a total of thirty-one units in ELSA (see Figure 2). Put simply, units consist of teaching objectives which are in some way closely associated with each other. Their primary purpose is to break down subject areas into smaller and more manageable components so as to enable the teacher to handle the materials in the classroom more easily.

Each unit has a topsheet which incorporates the following information:

a. A space for the pupil's name.
b. A list of skills a pupil should have prior to starting work on that unit (called entry skills).
c. A list of the teaching objectives in that unit in an abbreviated form.
d. A means of recording decisions taken about which objectives are to be taught and in what order.
e. A list of the materials required to assess that unit.

3. *Teaching objectives*

The thirty-one units each contain between two and nine teaching objectives. There is a total of one hundred and twenty-two objectives in ELSA. Look at the materials in Chapter 2. You will see that the teaching objectives are written under four columns headed: materials, instructions, pupil performance, and recommended criteria. In working with teachers over a number of years we have found this four-column format

Subject area	Units	Teaching objectives
ARITHMETIC	1. Numbers to 10	A1 to A5
pp. 9 to 25	2. Numerals to 10	A6 to A8
	3. Addition and subtraction to 10	A9 to A11
	4. Numbers 11 to 20	A12 to A14
	5. Numerals 11 to 20	A15 to A17
	6. Addition and subtraction to 20	A18 and A19
	7. Mixed addition and subtraction	A20 to A24
HANDWRITING	1. Letters and numerals	H1 to H3
pp. 27 to 30	2. Prose	H4 to H6
INDEPENDENCE SKILLS	1. Dressing	I1 to I5
pp. 31 to 41	2. Feeding and toileting	I6 to I9
	3. Orientation	I10 to I13
LANGUAGE	1. Naming	L1 to L6
pp. 43 to 66	2. Verbs	L7 to L9
	3. Same and different	L10 to L12
	4. Colours and shapes	L13 to L15
	5. Adverbs	L16 and L17
	6. Spatial concepts	L18 to L20
	7. Size and quantity	L21 to L23
	8. Opposites	L24 to L26
	9. Categories	L27 to L29
	10. Describing	L30 to L37
MOTOR SKILLS	1. Gross motor	M1 to M6
pp. 67 to 73	2. Fine motor	M7 to M10
READING	1. Sight vocabulary	R1 to R6
pp. 75 to 85	2. Reading books	R7 to R9
	3. Sounds and simple blends	R10 and R11
	4. Blends and combinations	R12 to R17
SPELLING	1. Basic vocabulary	S1 to S3
pp. 87 to 94	2. Sounds, blends, and combinations	S4 to S12
	3. Irregular words	S13 to S15

Figure 2: Summary of ELSA subject areas, units, and teaching objectives

to be the most popular. It allows a great deal of very detailed information to be included, but in such a way as to facilitate easy reference in the classroom.

You will also notice that each objective has a code (e.g. R7, M4) which appears in the extreme left-hand column of each page. The letter corresponds to the initial of the subject area. Thereafter the objectives are coded R1, R2, R3, and so on. Although this is emphasized later, please note that objectives are not necessarily taught in the order in which they are coded.

4. *Pupil records*

Pupil records are incorporated into the ELSA material. On the right-hand side of each page are four more columns headed: placement test, working on, mastered, and checked. Chapter 3 explains how the first of these is used to record details of the placement test and Chapter 6 describes the use of the other three in keeping continuous records of pupil progress.

5. *Assessment material*

The 'materials' column of each objective states the materials needed to assess that particular item. ELSA has been carefully designed to avoid, as much as possible, teachers having to spend time collecting together supplementary materials. In some items materials are described which should be readily available in most classrooms (e.g. paper, pencil, scissors). Where specially designed materials are required they are supplied in the final section of the book (called 'Assessment Material') on the page indicated on the unit topsheet.

In general, then, the assessment materials required when using ELSA are either readily available in the classroom or are provided in this book. We feel, however, that it is important that teachers should use ELSA flexibly, matching the teaching objectives closely to the curriculum of the school and the needs and interests of individual pupils. Consequently a proportion of the objectives necessitate teachers making additional materials.

In some of the reading and spelling items, for example, there is a need to decide upon the actual words to be learnt. These may be prescribed on the basis of lists of words taught within the school's spelling and reading schemes or, where teachers are committed to a language-experience approach, may consist of those words a child wishes to learn. Similarly, some of the language objectives have been left open so that the teacher can decide upon that content which is of most relevance to the individual pupil. Objectives L7 and L8, for example, focus on the pupil's use of verbs. There are ten common verbs in each and the materials required for their assessment are provided in the 'Assessment Material'. Objective L9 allows the teacher to specify ten other verbs of his or her own choice.

This flexibility has also been retained in dealing with the child's reading of books. Some schools rely on one reading scheme whilst others prefer to use books from a range of schemes. To allow for this objectives R7, R8, and R9 require the teacher to prepare assessment materials based upon the books being used in the class. Notes and examples explaining how this should be done are provided on pages 182 to 185.

Although additional materials will need to be produced before these particular objectives can be used in the classroom, their inclusion is important. They will add flexibility by allowing ELSA to be adapted to the needs and interests of *your* pupils.

Final comment

Do not worry if the ELSA materials appear rather complex at this stage. Chapters 3 to 6 provide a step-by-step explanation of how they should be used in the classroom. And remember, don't skip Chapter 2. Spend some time examining the material, reading each objective, and, where necessary, locating the appropriate assessment material.

2

ELSA

Teaching objectives in arithmetic, handwriting, independence skills, language, motor skills, reading, and spelling.

PUPIL RECORDS

Name____________________ Class_______ Date of birth____________

ELSA

Colour in units completed

ARITHMETIC	1	2	3	4	5	6	7
HANDWRITING	1	2					
INDEPENDENCE	1	2	3				
LANGUAGE	1	2	3	4	5	6	
	7	8	9	10			
MOTOR	1	2					
READING	1	2	3	4			
SPELLING	1	2	3				

ELSA	ARITHMETIC
UNIT **1**	NUMBERS TO 10

Child's Name ______________________________

ENTRY SKILLS: Repeat after teacher individual numbers

TEACHING OBJECTIVES:

A1	Counts aloud to 10	
A2	States cardinal property of sets of objects with between 0 and 10 items (linear)	
A3	States cardinal property of sets of objects with between 0 and 10 items (random)	
A4	States cardinal property of pictured sets with between 0 and 10 items	
A5	Constructs set of between 0 and 10 items	

MATERIALS REQUIRED:

Ten identical objects (eg bricks, straws or counters)
Pictured sets on pages 148 to 149

	Materials	Instructions	Pupil Performance	Recommended Criteria	Placement Test		Record (Date)		
							Working on	Mast-ered	Checked
A1	None	'Count up to 10.'	**Counts aloud to 10**	(10/10)	√	X			
A2	Present ten sets of between 0 and 10 identical objects (e.g. bricks, straws, counters), with items arranged in a straight line	For each set: 'How many are here?'	**States cardinal property of sets of objects with between 0 and 10 items** (linear arrangement)	(10/10)	√	X			
A3	Present ten sets of between 0 and 10 identical objects, with items in random spatial arrangement	For each set: 'How many are here?'	**States cardinal property of sets of objects with between 0 and 10 items** (random spatial arrangement)	(10/10)	√	X			

Notes/Comments

	Materials	Instructions	Pupil Performance	Recommended Criteria
A4	Ten pictured sets of between 0 and 10 items	For each picture: 'How many are here?'	**States cardinal property of pictured sets between 0 and 10 items**	(10/10)
A5	Ten identical objects	For each of ten numbers between 0 and 10: 'Give me____.'	**Constructs sets of between 0 and 10 items**	(10/10)

Placement Test		Record (Date)		
		Working on	Mastered	Checked
√	X			
√	X			

Notes/Comments

Child's Name ______________________

ELSA	ARITHMETIC
UNIT **2**	NUMERALS TO 10

ENTRY SKILLS: Match numerals; count to 10 (i.e. A1); and copy numerals legibly (not necessarily to criteria recommended in H2)

TEACHING OBJECTIVES:

A6	Reads aloud numerals 0 to 10	
A7	Writes numerals 0 to 10 from dictation	
A8	Writes cardinal property of sets with between 0 and 10 objects	

MATERIALS REQUIRED:

Numerals on page 150
Ten identical objects

	Materials	Instructions	Pupil Performance	Recommended Criteria	Place-ment Test		Record (Date)		
							Working on	Mast-ered	Checked
A6	Thirty numerals with 0 to 10 printed in random order two or three times each, presented for half a minute	'Read these numbers as quickly as you can, trying not to make any mistakes.'	**Reads aloud numbers 0 to 10**	50 per min Max. 2 errors	√	X			
A7	Paper and pencil	'Write down these numbers as I say them,' using ten numbers between 0 and 10 in random order	**Writes numerals 0 to 10 from dictation**	10/10	√	X			
A8	Five sets of between 0 and 10 identical objects Paper and pencil	For each set: 'Write down how many are here.'	**Writes cardinal property of sets with between 0 and 10 objects**	5/5	√	X			

Notes/Comments

Child's Name ______________________________

ELSA	ARITHMETIC
UNIT **3**	ADDITION AND SUBTRACTION TO 10

ENTRY SKILLS: Arithmetic Units 1 and 2

TEACHING OBJECTIVES:

A9	Adds two digits up to totals of 10 or less	
A10	Subtracts from 10 or less	
A11	Writes in missing number in addition sums to totals of 10 or less	

MATERIALS REQUIRED:

Copies of addition and subtraction sums on pages 151 to 153

	Materials	Instructions	Pupil Performance	Recommended Criteria	Placement Test		Record (Date)		
							Working on	Mastered	Checked
A9	Thirty different printed addition sums totalling 10 or less, presented for one minute	'Do these sums as quickly as you can, trying not to make any mistakes.'	**Adds two digits up to totals of 10 or less** (written response)	15 per min Max. 1 error	√	X			
A10	Thirty different printed subtraction sums from 10 or less, presented for one minute	'Do these sums as quickly as you can, trying not to make any mistakes.'	**Subtracts from 10 or less** (written response)	15 per min Max. 1 error	√	X			
A11	Thirty different printed addition sums with one number missing, presented for one minute	'Fill in the missing number in each of these sums. Work quickly, but try not to make mistakes.'	**Writes missing numbers in addition sums to totals of 10 or less**	10 per min Max. 1 error	√	X			

Notes/Comments To prevent a particular sequence of answers being memorized, the pupil can be given different starting points on the sheets of sums for A9 to A11

ELSA	ARITHMETIC
UNIT **4**	NUMBERS 11 TO 20

Child's Name ____________________

ENTRY SKILLS: Arithmetic Unit 1

TEACHING OBJECTIVES:

A12	Counts aloud from 11 to 20	
A13	States cardinal property of sets of objects with between 11 and 20 items	
A14	Constructs sets of between 11 and 20 items	

MATERIALS REQUIRED:

Twenty identical objects (e.g. straws, bricks, etc.)

	Materials	Instructions	Pupil Performance	Recommended Criteria	Placement Test		Record (Date)		
							Working on	Mastered	Checked
A12	None	'Count from 11 to 20.'	**Counts aloud from 11 to 20**	10/10	√	X			
A13	Present ten sets of between 11 and 20 identical objects, with items in random spatial arrangement	For each set: 'How many are here?'	**States cardinal property of sets of objects with between 11 and 20 items**	9/10	√	X			
A14	Twenty identical objects	For each number 11 to 20: 'Give me ____.'	**Constructs sets of between 11 and 20 items**	9/10	√	X			

Notes/Comments

ELSA	ARITHMETIC
UNIT **5**	NUMERALS 11 TO 20

Child's Name ______________________________

ENTRY SKILLS: Arithmetic Unit 2; count from 10 to 20 (i.e. A12)

TEACHING OBJECTIVES:

A15	Reads aloud numerals 11 to 20	
A16	Writes numerals 11 to 20 from dictation	
A17	Writes cardinal property of sets of between 11 and 20 objects	

MATERIALS REQUIRED:

Numerals on page 154
Twenty identical objects

	Materials	Instructions	Pupil Performance	Recommended Criteria	Placement Test		Record (Date) Working on	Mastered	Checked
A15	Thirty numerals with 11 to 20 printed in random order two or three times each, presented for half a minute	'Read these numbers as quickly as you can, trying not to make any mistakes.'	**Reads aloud numerals 11 to 20**	50 per min Max. 2 errors	√	X			
A16	Paper and pencil	'Write down these numbers as I say them,' using numbers 11 to 20 in random order	**Writes numerals 11 to 20 from dictation**	10/10	√	X			
A17	Five random sets of 11 to 20 identical objects Paper and pencil	For each set: 'Write down how many are here.'	**Writes cardinal property of sets of between 11 and 20 objects**	5/5	√	X			

Notes/Comments

Child's Name ______________________________

ELSA	ARITHMETIC
UNIT **6**	ADDITION AND SUBTRACTION TO 20

ENTRY SKILLS: Arithmetic Units 3, 4, and 5

TEACHING OBJECTIVES:

A18	Adds two numbers up to totals of 20 or less	
A19	Subtract from 20 or less	

MATERIALS REQUIRED:

Copies of addition and subtraction sums on pages 155 and 156

	Materials	Instructions	Pupil Performance	Recommended Criteria	Placement Test		Record (Date)		
							Working on	Mastered	Checked
					√	X			
A18	Thirty-two different printed addition sums totalling 20 or less, presented for one minute	'Do these sums as quickly as you can, trying not to make any mistakes.'	**Adds two numbers up to totals of 20 or less** (written response)	12 per min Max. 1 error					
A19	Thirty-two different printed subtraction sums from 20 or less, presented for one minute	'Do these sums as quickly as you can, trying not to make any mistakes.'	**Subtracts from 20 or less** (written response)	12 per min Max. 1 error					

Notes/Comments To prevent a particular sequence of answers being memorised, the pupil can be given different starting points on the sheets of sums for A18 and A19.

Child's Name ______________________________

ELSA	ARITHMETIC
UNIT **7**	MIXED ADDITION AND SUBTRACTION

ENTRY SKILLS: Arithmetic Unit 6

TEACHING OBJECTIVES:

A20	Adds up to, and subtracts from, 10 or less (written)	
A21	Adds up to, and subtracts from, 10 or less (verbal)	
A22	Adds up to, and subtracts from, 20 or less (written)	
A23	Adds three or four numbers up to totals of 20 or less (written)	
A24	Adds up to, and subtracts from, 20 or less (verbal)	

MATERIALS REQUIRED:

Sheets of sums on pages 157 to 159

	Materials	Instructions	Pupil Performance	Recommended Criteria	Placement Test		Record (Date)		
							Working on	Mastered	Checked
A20	Thirty different addition and subtraction sums to 10 or less, presented for one minute	'Do these sums as quickly as you can, trying not to make any mistakes.'	**Adds up to, and subtracts from 10 or less** (written response)	15 per min Max. 1 error	√	X			
A21	Ten different addition and subtraction sums to 10 or less, presented orally	'Tell me the answers to these sums.'	**Adds up to, and substracts from, 10 or less** (spontaneous verbal response)	10/10	√	X			
A22	Thirty-two mixed addition and subtraction sums to 20 or less, presented for one minute	'Do these sums as quickly as you can, trying not to make any mistakes.'	**Adds up to, and subtracts from, 20 or less** (written response)	12 per min Max. 1 error	√	X			

Notes/Comments

	Materials	Instructions	Pupil Performance	Recommended Criteria	Placement Test		Record (Date)		
							Working on	Mastered	Checked
A23	Twenty different addition sums of three or four numbers totalling 20 or less, presented for one minute	'Do these numbers as quickly as you can, trying not to make any mistakes.'	**Adds three or four numbers up to totals of 20 or less** (written response)	12 per min Max. 1 error	√	X			
A24	Ten different addition and subtraction sums to 20 or less, presented orally	'Tell me the answers to these sums.'	**Adds up to, and subtracts from, 20 or less** (spontaneous verbal response)	9/10	√	X			

Notes/Comments

ELSA	HANDWRITING
UNIT **1**	LETTERS AND NUMERALS

Child's Name ______________________________

ENTRY SKILLS: Hold pencil appropriately; copy horizontal, vertical, and circular lines

TEACHING OBJECTIVES:

H1	Copies lower case letters	
H2	Copies numerals 0 to 10	
H3	Copies capital letters	

MATERIALS REQUIRED:

Copies of letters and numerals on pages 160 to 162

	Materials	Instructions	Pupil Performance	Recommended Criteria	Placement Test		Record (Date)		
							Working on	Mast-ered	Checked
H1	Twenty-six lower case letters, with copying space below	'Copy each of these letters carefully.'	**Copies lower case letters legibly**	26/26	√	X			
H2	Numerals 0 to 9, each presented twice, with copying space below	'Copy each of these numbers carefully.'	**Copies numerals 0 to 10 legibly**	20/20	√	X			
H3	Twenty-six capital letters, with copying space below	'Copy each of these letters carefully.'	**Copies capital letters legibly**	26/26	√	X			

Notes/Comments 'Lines' may be added to the assessment material for H1 to H3 at the teacher's discretion.

Child's Name ________________________________

ELSA	HANDWRITING
UNIT **2**	PROSE

ENTRY SKILLS: Handwriting Unit 1

TEACHING OBJECTIVES:

H4	Copies prose from a model directly above	
H5	Copies prose from a model on separate paper	
H6	Copies prose from a model on a blackboard	

MATERIALS REQUIRED:

Writing samples on pages 163 to 165

	Materials	Instructions	Pupil Performance	Recommended Criteria	Placement Test		Record (Date)		
					√	X	Working on	Mastered	Checked
H4	Words in sentences with at least 50 letters and copying space below. Present for *two* minutes	'Copy these words quickly and carefully.'	**Copies prose from a model directly above,** legibly	20 per min Max. 2 errors					
H5	Words in sentences with at least 50 letters, and separate piece of paper. Present for *two* minutes	'Copy these words quickly and carefully on to this paper.'	**Copies prose from a model on a separate paper,** legibly	20 per min Max. 2 errors					
H6	Words in sentences with at least 50 letters, on blackboard between 2 and 4 yards from pupil, and piece of paper. Present for *two* minutes	'Copy these words quickly and carefully on to this paper.'	**Copies prose from a model on a blackboard,** legibly	20 per min Max. 2 errors					

Notes/Comments 'Lines' may be added to the assessment material for H4 to H6 at the teacher's discretion. Two samples are presented for H4 and three for H5.

ELSA INDEPENDENCE SKILLS	
UNIT **1**	DRESSING

Child's Name ____________________

ENTRY SKILLS: Pick up and hold articles of clothing

TEACHING OBJECTIVES:

I1	Removes clothes	
I2	Puts on clothes	
I3	Undoes and does up zip	
I4	Undoes and does up shoelaces	
I5	Undoes and does up four buttons	

MATERIALS REQUIRED:

Various items of clothing

	Materials	Instructions	Pupil Performance	Recommended Criteria	Placement Test	Record (Date) Working on	Mastered	Checked
I1	Two socks, two shoes, pants, vest, trousers (or skirt) and jumper	'Take off your clothes.'	**Removes clothes,** excluding difficult fastenings	8/8	√ X			
I2	Two socks, two shoes, pants, vest, trousers (or skirt) and jumper	'Put on your clothes.'	**Puts on clothes,** excluding difficult fastenings	8/8	√ X			
I3	Garment on with accessible zip	'Undo your zip… now do it up.'	**Undoes and does up zip**	2/2	√ X			

Notes/Comments

	Materials	Instructions	Pupil Performance	Recommended Criteria	Placement Test		Record (Date)		
							Working on	Mast-ered	Checked
I4	Shoes on with laces done up	'Undo your laces… now do them up.'	**Undoes and does up shoelaces**	4/4	√	X			
I5	Garment on with four accessible buttons done up	'Undo your buttons… now do them up.'	**Undoes and does up four buttons**	8/8	√	X			

Notes/Comments

Child's Name ____________________

ELSA INDEPENDENCE SKILLS	
UNIT 2	FEEDING AND TOILETING

ENTRY SKILLS: Pick up and hold utensils for 16 and 17; use toilet when taken for 18 and 19

TEACHING OBJECTIVES:

I6	Uses knife and fork	
I7	Drinks from cup	
I8	Remains clean and dry in school	
I9	Uses toilet independently	

MATERIALS REQUIRED:

Plate of food, and knife and fork
Cup
Suitable sized toilet

	Materials	Instructions	Pupil Performance	Recommended Criteria	Placement Test		Record (Date) Working on	Mastered	Checked
I6	Plate of food, knife and fork	None	**Uses knife and fork,** without spilling	1/1	√	X			
I7	Nearly full, ordinary cup	None	**Drinks from cup,** without spilling	1/1	√	X			

Notes/Comments

	Materials	Instructions	Pupil Performance	Recommended Criteria	Placement Test	Record (Date) Working on	Mastered	Checked
I8	None	None	**Remains clean and dry in school,** i.e. uses toilet as necessary for at least ten half days	10/10	√ X			
I9	None	None	**Uses toilet independently,** i.e. cleans self, flushes toilet, washes, and dries hands	4/4	√ X			

Notes/Comments

Child's Name ____________________

ELSA INDEPENDENCE SKILLS	
UNIT **3**	ORIENTATION

ENTRY SKILLS: Follow simple instructions

TEACHING OBJECTIVES:

I10	Points to own peg	
I11	Points to own drawer	
I12	Finds own classroom	
I13	Takes message to school office	

	Materials	Instructions	Pupil Performance	Recommended Criteria
I10	None	On two separate occasions: 'Where is your peg?'	**Points to own peg**	2/2
I11	None	On two separate occasions: 'Where is your drawer?'	**Points to own drawer**	2/2

Placement Test		Record (Date)		
		Working on	Mast-ered	Checked
√	X			
√	X			

Notes/Comments

	Materials	Instructions	Pupil Performance	Recommended Criteria	Placement Test √	Placement Test X	Record (Date) Working on	Mastered	Checked
I12	None	From playground, toilet, and school hall, say: 'Go to your classroom.'	**Finds own classroom**	3/3					
I13	Written message, register, etc.	On two separate occasions: 'Take this to (the secretary) and then come back.'	**Takes message to school office**	2/2					

Notes/Comments

ELSA	LANGUAGE
UNIT **1**	NAMING

Child's Name ______________________

ENTRY SKILLS: Repeat names of familiar objects

TEACHING OBJECTIVES:

L1	Names ten body parts	
L2	Names ten more body parts	
L3	Names ten articles of clothing	
L4	Names ten more articles of clothing from pictures	
L5	Names ten classroom objects	
L6	Names ten more classroom objects from pictures	

MATERIALS REQUIRED:

Clothing in L3
Classroom objects in L5
Pictures on pages 166 to 167

	Materials	Instructions	Pupil Performance	Recommended Criteria	Placement Test		Record (Date)		
							Working on	Mastered	Checked
L1	None	Pointing to parts of child's body (i.e. arm, face, hand, nose, foot, head, leg, finger, chin, eyes: 'What's this?'	**Names ten body parts**	10/10	√	X			
L2	None	Pointing to body parts (i.e. teeth, knee, cheek, wrist, toe, hair, neck, ankle, shoulder, elbow): 'What's this?'	**Names ten more body parts**	10/10	√	X			
L3	None	Pointing to articles of clothing (i.e. shirt, trousers, shoes, socks, dress, skirt, coat, hat, gloves, sweater): 'What's this?'	**Names ten articles of clothing**	10/10	√	X			

Notes/Comments

	Materials	Instructions	Pupil Performance	Recommended Criteria	Placement Test		Record (Date)		
							Working on	Mastered	Checked
L4	Pictures of clothing (i.e. pyjamas, zip, button, boots, handkerchief, tie, belt, vest, scarf, shorts)	For each picture: 'What's this?'	**Names ten more articles of clothing from pictures**	10/10	√	X			
L5	Ten classroom objects (i.e. book, blackboard, desk, rubber, pencil, chalk, bin, paint, chair, picture)	Pointing to each object: 'What's this?'	**Names ten classroom objects**	10/10	√	X			
L6	Pictures of ten classroom objects (i.e. pencil, scissors, clock, table, door, ruler, crayon, ball, drawer, sink)	Pointing to each picture: 'What's this?'	**Names ten more classroom objects from pictures**	10/10	√	X			

Notes/Comments

Child's Name ______________________________

ELSA	LANGUAGE
UNIT **2**	VERBS

ENTRY SKILLS: Speak in simple sentences; repeat verbs

TEACHING OBJECTIVES:

L7	Uses ten verbs	
L8	Uses ten more verbs	
L9	Uses ten other verbs	

MATERIALS REQUIRED:

Pictures on pages 168 to 173

	Materials	Instructions	Pupil Performance	Recommended Criteria	Placement Test		Record (Date)		
							Working on	Mastered	Checked
L7	Pictures illustrating ten verbs (i.e. clap, dance, drink, jump, eat, swing, cry, play, ride, shout)	For each picture: 'What's happening here?'	**Uses ten verbs** (e.g. He's clapping)	10/10	√	X			
L8	Pictures illustrating ten verbs (i.e. blow, slide, climb, catch, fly, hop, kick, pull, push, drag)	For each picture: 'What's happening here?'	**Uses ten more verbs**	10/10	√	X			
L9	Pictures illustrating the following ten verbs: ________ ________ ________	For each picture: 'What's happening here?'	**Uses ten other verbs**	10/10	√	X			

Notes/Comments

ELSA	LANGUAGE
UNIT **3**	SAME AND DIFFERENT

Child's Name ____________________

ENTRY SKILLS: Match colours, shapes, and by size, after demonstration

TEACHING OBJECTIVES:

L10	States whether colours are same or different	
L11	States whether shapes are same or different	
L12	States whether objects are same or different in size	

MATERIALS REQUIRED:

Five pairs of objects in L10
Five pairs of shapes in L11
Five pairs of objects in L12

	Materials	Instructions	Pupil Performance	Recommended Criteria	Placement Test		Record (Date)		
							Working on	Mast-ered	Checked
L10	Five pairs of similar objects: two pairs of same colour	For each pair: 'Are these the same colour or different?'	**States whether colours are same or different**	5/5	√	X			
L11	Five pairs of shapes; two pairs the same	For each pair: 'Are these shapes the same or different?'	**States whether shapes are same or different**	5/5	√	X			
L12	Five pairs of similar objects: two pairs the same size	For each pair: 'Are these the same size or different?'	**States whether objects are same or different in size**	5/5	√	X			

Notes/Comments

ELSA	LANGUAGE
UNIT 4	COLOURS AND SHAPES

Child's Name ____________________

ENTRY SKILLS: Matches colours and shapes, after demonstration

TEACHING OBJECTIVES:

L13	Names five colours	
L14	Names five more colours	
L15	Names five shapes	

MATERIALS REQUIRED:

Ten coloured objects
Five shapes

	Materials	Instructions	Pupil Performance	Recommended Criteria	Placement Test		Record (Date)		
							Working on	Mastered	Checked
L13	Five coloured objects (i.e. red, yellow, blue, black, white)	'Tell me these colours.'	**Names five colours**	5/5	√	X			
L14	Five coloured objects (i.e. green, purple, orange, brown, pink)	'Tell me these colours.'	**Names five more colours**	5/5	√	X			
L15	Five shapes (i.e. square, circle, triangle, rectangle, diamond)	'Tell me these shapes.'	**Names five shapes**	5/5	√	X			

Notes/Comments

Child's Name ______________________________

ELSA	LANGUAGE
UNIT **5**	ADVERBS

ENTRY SKILLS: Language Unit 2

TEACHING OBJECTIVES:

L16	Uses five adverbs	
L17	Uses five other adverbs	

	Materials	Instructions	Pupil Performance	Recommended Criteria	Placement Test		Record (Date) Working on	Mastered	Checked
					√	X			
L16	None	Teacher demonstrates: 'I am walking slowly… Now how am I walking?' (i.e. walking quickly, softly, loudly, happily, sadly)	**Uses five adverbs** (e.g. 'You are walking quickly.')	5/5					
L17	None	Demonstrate the following five adverbs: ______ ______ 'How am I ____?'	**Uses five other adverbs**	5/5					

Notes/Comments

Child's Name ______________________

ELSA	LANGUAGE
UNIT 6	SPATIAL CONCEPTS

ENTRY SKILLS: Language Units 1 and 2

TEACHING OBJECTIVES:

L18	Uses five spatial concepts	
L19	Uses five more spatial concepts	
L20	Uses five other spatial concepts	

MATERIALS REQUIRED:

Pictures on pages 174 to 175

	Materials	Instructions	Pupil Performance	Recommended Criteria	Placement Test		Record (Date)		
					√	X	Working on	Mastered	Checked
L18	Pictures illustrating five spatial concepts (i.e. on, in, under, next to, in front of)	For each picture: 'Where is the____?'	**Uses five spatial concepts**	5/5					
L19	Pictures illustrating five spatial concepts (i.e. behind, between, near, over, inside)	For each picture: 'Where is the ____?'	**Uses five more spatial concepts**	5/5					
L20	Pictures illustrating the following five spatial concepts: ____________ ____________ ____________	For each picture: 'Where is the ____?'	**Uses five other spatial concepts**	5/5					

Notes/Comments

Child's Name ______________________________

ELSA	LANGUAGE
UNIT **7**	SIZE AND QUANTITY

ENTRY SKILLS: Language Unit 3

TEACHING OBJECTIVES:

L21	Uses four size concepts	
L22	Uses five quantitative concepts	
L23	Uses five other quantitative concepts	

MATERIALS REQUIRED:

Bricks or blocks of assorted size

	Materials	Instructions	Pupil Performance	Recommended Criteria	Placement Test		Record (Date) Working on	Mastered	Checked
L21	Bricks or blocks of the same colour but assorted size	After demonstration: 'Tell me the missing words: This one is ___ (big). This one is ___ (small). This one is ___ (short). This one is ___ (long).'	**Uses four size concepts**	4/4	√	X			
L22	Up to ten bricks or blocks arranged appropriately for each item	After demonstration: 'Tell me the missing words: I have ___ than you (more). You have ___ than me (less). I have them ___ (all). You have a ___ (lot). I have a ___ (few).'	**Uses five quantitative concepts**	5/5	√	X			
L23	Groups of suitable objects	After demonstration: 'Tell me the missing words.' Sentences to illustrate the following five terms: ___________ ___________	**Uses five other quantitative concepts**	5/5	√	X			

Notes/Comments During placement testing only, instructions should be preceded by a demonstration of the use of the concepts to be elicited, using the assessment materials.

Child's Name ______________________________

ELSA	LANGUAGE
UNIT **8**	OPPOSITES

ENTRY SKILLS: Language Units 6 and 7

TEACHING OBJECTIVES:

L24	States five opposites	
L25	States five more opposites	
L26	States five other opposites	

	Materials	Instructions	Pupil Performance	Recommended Criteria	Placement Test		Record (Date) Working on	Mastered	Checked
L24	None	'The opposite of down is up, tell me the opposites of these words: hot (cold), good (bad), wet (dry), fat (thin), new (old).'	**States five opposites**	5/5	√	X			
L25	None	'Tell me the opposites of these words: sweet (sour), strong (weak), wrong (right), heavy (light), ugly (pretty).'	**States five more opposites**	5/5	√	X			
L26	None	'Tell me the opposites of these words:' ____________ ____________ ____________	**States five other opposites**	5/5	√	X			

Notes/Comments

Child's Name ______________________________

ELSA	LANGUAGE
UNIT 9	CATEGORIES

ENTRY SKILLS: Language Unit 3 and Objective L22 (in Language Unit 7); name items in each picture

TEACHING OBJECTIVES:

L27	Uses five category words	
L28	Uses five more category words	
L29	Uses five other category words	

MATERIALS REQUIRED:

Pictures on pages 176 to 179

	Materials	Instructions	Pupil Performance	Recommended Criteria	Placement Test		Record (Date)		
							Working on	Mastered	Checked
L27	Pictures of clothes, animals, fruit, numbers, toys	For each picture: 'How are all these the same?'	**Uses five category words** (e.g. 'They are animals'.)	5/5	√	X			
L28	Pictures of furniture, tools, vehicles, insects, vegetables	For each picture: 'How are all these the same?'	**Uses five more category words** (e.g. 'They are tools.')	5/5	√	X			
L29	Pictures of the following five categories: ______ ______ ______	For each picture: 'How are all these the same?'	**Uses five other category words**	5/5	√	X			

Notes/Comments

ELSA	LANGUAGE
UNIT 10	DESCRIBING

Child's Name ______________________

ENTRY SKILLS: Language Units 8 and 9

TEACHING OBJECTIVES:

L30	Describes two features of each of five objects	
L31	Describes two features of each of five other objects	
L32	Describes the functions of five objects	
L33	Describes the functions of five more objects	
L34	Describes how to carry out five tasks	
L35	Describes how to carry out five other tasks	
L36	Describes similarities and differences of five pairs of objects	
L37	Describes similarities and differences of five other pairs of objects	

MATERIALS REQUIRED:

Pictures on page 180

	Materials	Instructions	Pupil Performance	Recommended Criteria	Placement Test		Record (Date) Working on	Mastered	Checked
					√	X			
L30	Five objects (i.e. pencil, chair, cup, apple, watch)	For each object: 'Tell me two things about this (pencil).'	**Describes two features of each of five objects** (e.g. size, shape, function, colour, etc.)	10/10					
L31	The following five objects: ___ ___ ___	For each object: 'Tell me two things about this(____).'	**Describes two features of each of five other objects**	10/10					
L32	Five objects (i.e. scissors, spoon, toothbrush, belt, handkerchief)	For each object: 'What is this used for?'	**Describes the functions of five objects** (e.g. 'It's used for cutting paper.')	5/5					

Notes/Comments

	Materials	Instructions	Pupil Performance	Recommended Criteria	Placement Test		Record (Date) Working on	Mastered	Checked
L33	The following five objects: __________ __________ __________	For each object: 'What is this used for?'	**Describes the functions of five other objects**	5/5	√	X			
L34	None	For each of five tasks (i.e. washing hands, dressing, painting a picture, going to the school office, playing a drum) 'Tell me how to ____.'	**Describes how to carry out five tasks,** each description to include at least two verbs	10/10	√	X			
L35	None	For each of the following five tasks: __________ __________ __________	**Describes how to carry out five other tasks,** each description to include at least two verbs	10/10	√	X			

Notes/Comments

	Materials	Instructions	Pupil Performance	Recommended Criteria	Placement Test		Record (Date)		
							Working on	Mast-ered	Checked
L36	Pictures of five pairs of objects (i.e. canoe/boat, deckchair/easy chair, coat/dress, car/bus, cup/glass	For each picture: 'How are they the same?... How are they different?'	**Describes similarities and differences of five pairs of objects** (i.e. one of each)	10/10	√	X			
L37	Pictures of the following five pairs of objects: ____________ ____________	For each picture: 'How are they the same: ... How are they different?'	**Describes similarities and differences of five other pairs of objects** (i.e. one of each)	10/10	√	X			

Notes/Comments

Child's Name ______________________

ELSA	MOTOR SKILLS
UNIT **1**	GROSS MOTOR

ENTRY SKILLS: Walk and run independently; pick up a ball

TEACHING OBJECTIVES:

M1	Walks up four school stairs	
M2	Walks down four school stairs	
M3	Runs between skittles	
M4	Kicks stationary ball	
M5	Throws small ball	
M6	Bounces and catches small ball	

MATERIALS REQUIRED:

Four school stairs
Six skittles
Large and small ball

	Materials	Instructions	Pupil Performance	Recommended Criteria	Placement Test		Record (Date)		
							Working on	Mastered	Checked
					√	X			
M1	At least four stairs	'Walk upstairs.'	**Walks up four school stairs,** alternating feet	4/4					
M2	At least four stairs	'Walk downstairs.'	**Walks down four school stairs,** alternating feet	4/4					
M3	Line of six skittles, each 6 ft apart	After demonstration: 'Run between the skittles.'	**Runs between skittles,** without missing a gate or knocking over a skittle	6/6					

Notes/Comments

	Materials	Instructions	Pupil Performance	Recommended Criteria	Placement Test		Record (Date)		
							Working on	Mastered	Checked
M4	A 5 in diameter ball, presented five times	'Kick the ball to me'	**Kicks stationary ball,** at least 12 feet	5/5	√	X			
M5	A small ball (e.g. tennis ball), presented five times	'Throw the ball to me.'	**Throws small ball,** at least 12 feet	5/5	√	X			
M6	A small ball (e.g. tennis ball), presented five times	'Bounce this ball and catch it.'	**Bounces and catches small ball**	10/10	√	X			

Notes/Comments

Child's Name ______________________________

ELSA	MOTOR SKILLS
UNIT **2**	FINE MOTOR

ENTRY SKILLS: Hold a pencil and scissors appropriately

TEACHING OBJECTIVES:

M7	Folds paper	
M8	Cuts paper with scissors	
M9	Copies square, circle, and triangle	
M10	Colours in square, circle, and triangle	

MATERIALS REQUIRED:

15 cm square of paper with line down the middle
15 cm square of paper with two lines 2 cm apart down the middle
Scissors
Pictures of shapes on page 181

	Materials	Instructions	Pupil Performance	Recommended Criteria	Place-ment Test		Record (Date)		
							Working on	Mast-ered	Checked
M7	15 cm square of paper with line drawn down the middle, presented five times	'Fold the paper along the line.'	**Folds paper**, to within approx. 1 cm of either side of line	4/5	√	X			
M8	15 cm square of paper with lines drawn down the middle, 2 cm apart, presented five times. Scissors	'Cut the paper between these lines.'	**Cuts paper with scissors,** without breaking the lines	4/5	√	X			

Notes/Comments

	Materials	Instructions	Pupil Performance	Recommended Criteria	Placement Test		Record (Date) Working on	Mastered	Checked
M9	Pictures of circle, square, and triangle, each presented twice. Paper and pencil	'Copy these shapes on your paper.'	**Copies circle, square, and triangle**	6/6	√	X			
M10	Outline of 2 in diameter circle, 2 in square, and 2 in triangle, each presented twice. Coloured pencils	'Colour in these shapes without going outside the lines.'	**Colours in circle, square, and triangle,** without breaking the outline	6/6	√	X			

Notes/Comments

ELSA	READING
UNIT **1**	SIGHT VOCABULARY

Child's Name ____________________

ENTRY SKILLS: Reads aloud two out of three words of own choice, learned 24 hours earlier

TEACHING OBJECTIVES:

R1	Reads aloud ten words	
R2	Builds and reads aloud three sentences	
R3	Reads aloud twenty words	
R4	Builds and reads aloud five sentences	
R5	Reads aloud forty words	
R6	Builds and reads aloud ten sentences	

MATERIALS REQUIRED:

Twenty flash cards of teacher's (or pupils') choice
Sheet of forty words

	Materials	Instructions	Pupil Performance	Recommended Criteria	Placement Test	Record (Date): Working on	Record (Date): Mastered	Record (Date): Checked
R1	The following ten words each presented on an individual flash card: ______ ______ ______	'Read these words aloud.'	**Reads aloud ten words**	10/10	√ / X			
R2	The ten flash cards from R1, presented three times	'Use these words to make a sentence … What does it say:' Dismantle the sentence and repeat	**Builds and reads aloud three sentences,** each containing at least three words	3/3	√ / X			
R3	The ten words from R1, plus the following ten words, each presented on an individual flashcard: ______ ______ ______	'Read these words aloud.'	**Reads aloud twenty words**	20/20	√ / X			

Notes/Comments In this unit placement testing should be discontinued at the discretion of the teacher.

	Materials	Instructions	Pupil Performance	Recommended Criteria	Placement Test	Record (Date) Working on	Mastered	Checked
R4	The twenty flash cards from R3, presented five times	'Use these words to make a sentence … What does it say?' Dismantle the sentence and repeat	**Builds and reads aloud five sentences,** each containing at least four words	5/5	√ X			
R5	A sheet with the twenty words from R3 plus the following 20 words: __________ __________ __________	'Read these words aloud.'	**Reads aloud forty words**	38/40	√ X			
R6	The sheet of forty words from R5, presented five times	'Use these words to make a sentence. … What does it say?' Dismantle the sentence and repeat	**Builds and reads aloud ten sentences,** each containing at least four words	5/5	√ X			

Notes/Comments

Child's Name ______________________________

ELSA	READING
UNIT 2	READING BOOKS

ENTRY SKILLS: For first book, an appropriate sight vocabulary; for subsequent books, mastery of previous book, or books, in the school scheme

TEACHING OBJECTIVES:

BOOK TITLE: ______________		
R7	Reads aloud new words	
R8	Reads aloud passage	
R9	Answers oral comprehension questions	
BOOK TITLE: ______________		
R7	Reads aloud new words	
R8	Reads aloud passage	
R9	Answers oral comprehension questions	
BOOK TITLE: ______________		
R7	Reads aloud new words	
R8	Reads aloud passage	
R9	Answers oral comprehension questions	

MATERIALS REQUIRED:

For examples and notes see pages 182 to 185

	Materials	Instructions	Pupil Performance	Recommended Criteria	Place-ment Test		Record (Date)		
					√	X	Working on	Mast-ered	Checked
R7	New words from current reading book printed on a sheet, repeated as necessary to 30. Present for half a minute.	'Read these words as quickly as you can, trying not to make mistakes.'	**Reads aloud new words from** __________	40 per min Max. 2 errors					
R8	A hundred-word passage from current reading book printed on a sheet without illustrations. Present for one minute	'Read this story as quickly as you can, trying not to make mistakes.'	**Reads aloud passage from** __________	70 per min Max. 2 errors					
R9	Passage from R8, plus five appropriate comprehension questions	'After you have read this story to yourself, I am going to ask you these questions. Listen carefully ...' Read out all five questions. Repeat them individually *after* pupil has read the passage	**Answers oral comprehension questions on passage from** __________	5/5					

Notes/Comments For examples of materials cited in R7, R8 and R9 see pages 184 to 187.

Child's Name ______________________________

ELSA	READING
UNIT 3	SOUNDS AND SIMPLE BLENDS

ENTRY SKILLS: An appropriate sight vocabulary (usually between fifty and a hundred words)

TEACHING OBJECTIVES:

R10	Reads aloud short letter sounds	
R11	Reads aloud consonant–vowel–consonant words	

MATERIALS REQUIRED:

Sheets of letters and words on pages 186 and 187

	Materials	Instructions	Pupil Performance	Recommended Criteria	Placement Test		Record (Date) Working on	Mastered	Checked
					√	X			
R10	Twenty-six lower case letters each presented randomly twice on a sheet. Present for one minute	'Read these sounds quickly, trying not to make mistakes.'	**Reads aloud short letter sounds**	40 per min Max. 2 errors					
R11	Sixty different C–V–C words with each vowel used twelve times, presented for one minute	'Read these words quickly, trying not to make mistakes.'	**Reads aloud consonant – vowel – consonant words**	40 per min max. 2 errors					

Notes/Comments

Child's Name ______________________________

ELSA	READING
UNIT **4**	BLENDS AND COMBINATIONS

ENTRY SKILLS: Reading Unit 3

TEACHING OBJECTIVES:

R12	Reads aloud words with common final consonant blends	
R13	Reads aloud words with common initial consonant blends	
R14	Reads aloud words with final 'e'	
R15	Reads aloud words with letter combinations	
R16	Reads aloud words with more letter combinations	
R17	Reads aloud words with other letter combinations	

MATERIALS REQUIRED:

Sheets of words on pages 188 to 192

	Materials	Instructions	Pupil Performance	Recommended Criteria	Placement Test		Record (Date) Working on	Mastered	Checked
R12	Sixty different C–V–C–C words, presented for one minute	'Read these words quickly, trying not to make mistakes.'	**Reads aloud words with common final consonant blends**	40 per min Max. 2 errors	√	X			
R13	Sixty different C–C–V–C words, presented for one minute	'Read these words quickly, trying not to make mistakes.'	**Reads aloud words with common initial consonant blends**	40 per min Max. 2 errors	√	X			
R14	Sixty different words with final 'e', presented for one minute	'Read these words quickly, trying not to make mistakes.'	**Reads aloud words with final 'e'**	40 per min Max. 2 errors	√	X			

Notes/Comments

	Materials	Instructions	Pupil Performance	Recommended Criteria	Placement Test		Record (Date)		
					√	X	Working on	Mastered	Checked
R15	Sixty different words with letter combinations (i.e. ai, ng, th, sh, ea, ur), presented for one minute	'Read these words quickly, trying not to make mistakes.'	**Reads aloud words with letter combinations**	40 per min Max. 2 errors					
R16	Sixty different words with letter combinations (i.e. ar, oo, ch, ou, ee, or), presented for one minute	'Read these words quickly, trying not to make mistakes.'	**Reads aloud words with more letter combinations**	40 per min Max. 2 errors					
R17	Sixty different words with the following letter combinations: __________ __________ Present for one minute	'Read these words quickly, trying not to make mistakes.'	**Reads aloud words with other letter combinations**	40 per min Max. 2 errors					

Notes/Comments

Child's Name ______________________________

ELSA	SPELLING
UNIT 1	BASIC VOCABULARY

ENTRY SKILLS: R1 for S1; R3 for S2; and R5 for S3

TEACHING OBJECTIVES:

S1	Writes ten words from dictation	
S2	Writes ten more words from dictation	
S3	Writes ten more words from dictation	

MATERIALS REQUIRED:

Word lists from R1, R3, and R5

	Materials	Instructions	Pupil Performance	Recommended Criteria	Placement Test		Record (Date) Working on	Mastered	Checked
					√	X			
S1	List of ten words from R1. Paper and pencil	'Write down these words: ______.'	**Writes ten words from dictation**	9/10					
S2	List of ten *new* words from R3. Paper and pencil	'Write down these words: ______.'	**Writes ten more words from dictation**	9/10					
S3	List of ten of the words from R5. Paper and pencil	'Write down these words: ______.'	**Writes ten more words from dictation**	9/10					

Notes/Comments

Child's Name ____________________

ELSA	SPELLING
UNIT **2**	SOUNDS, BLENDS, AND COMBINATIONS

ENTRY SKILLS: Reading Unit 3; attention must also be paid to the relationship with individual objectives in Reading Unit 4

TEACHING OBJECTIVES:

S4	Writes letter sounds from dictation	
S5	Writes ten consonant–vowel–consonant words from dictation	
S6	Writes ten more consonant–vowel–consonant words from dictation	
S7	Writes ten words with common final consonant blends from dictation	
S8	Writes ten more words with common final consonant blends from dictation	
S9	Writes ten words with common initial consonant blends from dictation	
S10	Writes ten more words with common initial consonant blends from dictation	
S11	Writes ten words with final 'e' from dictation	
S12	Writes ten more words with final 'e' from dictation	

MATERIALS REQUIRED:

Sheets of words from pages 187 to 190

	Materials	Instructions	Pupil Performance	Recommended Criteria	Placement Test		Record (Date) Working on	Mastered	Checked
					√	X			
S4	Paper and pencil	'Write down these sounds …b, as in ball.' Present letter sounds in random order.	**Writes letter sounds from dictation**	26/26					
S5	The following ten words from R11: ____ ____ ____ Paper and pencil	'Write down these words: ____'	**Writes ten consonant – vowel – consonant words from dictation**	9/10					
S6	The following ten words from R11: ____ ____ ____ Paper and pencil	'Write down these words ____'	**Writes ten more consonant – vowel – consonant words from dictation**	9/10					

Notes/Comments

	Materials	Instructions	Pupil Performance	Recommended Criteria	Placement Test		Record (Date) Working on	Mastered	Checked
					√	X			
S7	The following ten words from R12: ________ ________ ________ Paper and pencil	'Write down these words: ________'	**Writes ten words with common final consonant blends from dictation**	9/10					
S8	The following ten words from R12: ________ ________ ________ Paper and pencil	'Write down these words: ________'	**Writes ten more words with common final consonant blends from dictation**	9/10					
S9	The following ten words from R13: ________ ________ ________ Paper and pencil	'Write down these words: ________'	**Writes ten words with common initial blends from dictation**	9/10					

Notes/Comments

	Materials	Instructions	Pupil Performance	Recommended Criteria	Placement Test		Record (Date)		
							Working on	Mastered	Checked
S10	The following ten words from R13: __________ __________ __________ Paper and pencil	'Write down these words: __________'	**Writes ten more words with common initial consonant blends from dictation**	9/10	√	X			
S11	The following ten words from R14: __________ __________ __________ Paper and pencil	'Write down these words: __________'	**Writes ten words with final 'e' from dictation**	9/10	√	X			
S12	The following ten words from R14: __________ __________ __________ Paper and pencil	'Write down these words: __________'	**Writes ten more words with final 'e' from dictation**	9/10	√	X			

Notes/Comments

Child's Name ____________________

ELSA	SPELLING
UNIT **3**	IRREGULAR WORDS

ENTRY SKILLS: Reads aloud words to be spelt

TEACHING OBJECTIVES:

S13	Writes ten irregular words from dictation	
S14	Writes ten more irregular words from dictation	
S15	Writes ten other irregular words from dictation	

MATERIALS REQUIRED:

List of recommended words on page 193

	Materials	Instructions	Pupil Performance	Recommended Criteria	Placement Test	Record (Date) Working on	Mastered	Checked
S13	The following ten words selected from page____ __________ __________ __________ Paper and pencil	'Write down these words: __________'	**Writes ten irregular words from dictation**	10/10	√ X			
S14	The following ten words selected from page____ __________ __________ __________ Paper and pencil	'Write down these words: __________'	**Writes ten more irregular words from dictation**	10/10	√ X			
S15	The following ten words selected from page____ __________ __________ __________ Paper and pencil	'Write down these words: __________'	**Writes ten other irregular words from dictation**	10/10	√ X			

Notes/Comments

3

The Placement Test

To provide detailed guidelines on how to use the ELSA placement test in the classroom.

Points to check first

There are three basic checks which should be made on any pupil who is seen to be having difficulties in school before using ELSA:

1. Can the pupil hear properly?
2. Can he see properly?
3. Is there any medical condition or prescribed medication which might be adversely affecting his performance in school?

Hearing deficits in young children can be extremely difficult to detect. For example, they might be intermittent (i.e. come and go over a few days), and they can be manifested in behaviour which is typical of slow learning pupils. We have known many children who have been reported as having retarded speech and language development, or of being unable to make friends or follow simple instructions in the classroom. The root cause of these problems can be — often to the amazement of parents and teachers — that the pupil simply cannot hear much of what is said to him.

Although a thorough audiometric investigation is a technical business, schools should be an important part of any screening procedure. Merely being alert to the possibility of a hearing deficit is an important contribution. If you are uncertain it is better to be safe than sorry. Ask your headteacher to arrange for the pupil's hearing to be tested. The parents' permission for this ought to be sought. Remember too that the problem may be intermittent, and so don't be afraid to ask for a second test if subsequently you are not satisfied.

Poor vision is usually less well disguised in young children but again, if a pupil is having a problem in learning, you should make sure that this is not because he is having difficulty seeing what he is being asked to do. As with hearing, the parents should be contacted first and either an appointment made to see a private optician or the appropriate person in the School Health Service notified of your concern.

The third point can be clarified by the family GP in liaison with the pupil's parents. The GP will be able to confirm whether the child suffers from any medical condition, or is taking medication, which is likely to affect adversely his performance in school.

These last few paragraphs are not specifically to do with ELSA, but they are extremely important. Try to memorise the three points — hearing, vision and medical condition — and always bear in mind that one of these might be causing the problem.

The purpose of the placement test

The sole purpose of the placement test is: *To find out what the pupil can and cannot do.*

The placement test does no more than this. Think for a moment how important this information is. It doesn't matter who is teaching, who is learning or what is being taught, the most important information the teacher can have is what the learner already knows. If you do not know this, you do not know where to begin teaching.

We assume that the teacher already has a reasonable knowledge of the pupil and his educational attainments. Indeed this is a requirement of the teacher who is to use ELSA. For example, deciding which subject areas to use with which pupils requires the teacher to know something of each pupil's strengths and weaknesses. If you are not the child's teacher but still wish to use ELSA, we recommend that you spend some time observing the pupil during normal classroom activities and gather as much information as possible about the work he has been doing.

Using teaching objectives for assessment

What follows is a description of a procedure for assessing any *one* of ELSA's one hundred and twenty two teaching objectives. It has to be carried out with the individual pupil, but should literally take only one to three minutes. Details concerning where and when to test appear later, but for the reader who is prone to panic it should be stressed now that at no point do we suggest that the placement test should be administered in its entirety.

The procedure is as follows:-

1. Present the materials described in the 'Materials' column.
2. Give the instructions provided in the 'Instructions' column.
3. Observe the 'Pupil performance'.
4. See if it reaches the 'Recommended criteria'.
5. Record the details of the pupil's performance in the 'Placement test' column.

The procedure is simple and quick. There follows some brief explanatory notes on each of these five stages.

1. *Materials*

The materials described in most of the ELSA teaching objectives, you will recall, either appear in the Assessment Material or should be readily available in the classroom. A few of the objectives require no materials and some require materials to be produced. *Before testing make sure that you have in front of you all the materials you are going to need.* If you intend assessing more than one objective, you should try to move smoothly from one activity to the next. To do so you must have the material ready and the pages in the Assessment Material identified so that they can be found and turned to without fuss.

2. *Instructions*

The teacher's instructions in ELSA have been carefully scripted to provide simple, easy-to-understand statements and questions. These instructions have been tried and tested in the classroom and they seem to work well with most children.

Three simple and perhaps obvious points:

a. Try to sound as if the 'lines' are yours and are not being read from a book.
b. Remember to speak clearly.
c. 'Soften' the instructions by frequently prefacing questions with the pupil's name.

3. *Pupil peformance*

The descriptions in the 'Pupil Performance' column have been very carefully worded. You will notice that in each there is a verb which describes an action which can be observed *directly*. In other words, we have avoided 'fuzzy' verbs like 'thinks', 'understands' and 'knows' which require the teacher to read the pupil's mind. This point should be borne in mind if you change any of the ELSA teaching objectives or write some of your own to supplement ELSA.

By this stage, therefore, you have presented the material and given the instruction. *Now you simply observe*. Does the pupil do what is described in the Pupil Performance column?

4. *Recommended criteria*

Curriculum material in most schools very rarely specify clear criteria. It is important to do so for a number of reasons. It avoids pupils moving on to more difficult work too early. How often are pupils given Book 3 in a reading scheme before Book 2 can be read properly? Or asked to add numbers to twenty before they can add single digits to ten reliably? Moreover the standard of performance achieved on a particular skill effects the likelihood of it being retained over a period of time. For these and other reasons described in detail later this aspect of ELSA is felt to be of crucial importance. Considerable care should therefore be taken to record details of the pupil's performance in the manner described below.

There are two different kinds of criteria used in ELSA:

a. *Accuracy* e.g. 9/10. In these objectives (examples include A1 to A4 on page 10) we are concerned simply with the number of correct responses made by the pupil, expressed as a fraction of the maximum possible score. During the placement test, therefore, using a pencil and paper, you should *note the number of correct and incorrect responses made.*
b. *Fluency* e.g. 15 per min, max. 1 error. Fluency is a combination of accuracy *and* speed. In ELSA such criteria are expressed as responses *per minute*. This kind of criteria is particularly important in subjects like reading where pupils need to work on both aspects of their performance.

In most of the ELSA objectives which have a fluency criteria, the materials are presented for *one* minute, and it is then simply a matter of noting the number of correct and incorrect responses made in that time. Examples of this type include A9 to A11 and R12 to R17.

In a small number of objectives the length of time which the pupil is given to perform the task is *not* one minute. When this occurs the time allowed is indicated in the materials column. In A6 on page 14, for example, a sheet of numbers is presented to the pupil for only half a minute but the recommended criteria is '50 per min. Max 2 errors'. In such cases it is necessary to convert the pupil's performance to correct and incorrect responses *per minute*. This can be done very simply — in this instance, obviously, by doubling the number of correct and incorrect responses made in half minute. Working in responses per minute also facilitates the use of more advanced measurement procedures which are described in Chapter 7.

5. *Recording the results*

In the light of the notes provided on giving a placement test, recording results needs little additional explanation. Quite simply, you record in the spaces provided the number of correct *and* incorrect responses made by the pupil — whether the recommended criteria is of the accuracy or fluency kind. At the top of the box there is space to record the date on which the placement test was given.

Date:	
✓	×

Placement Test Entry

You will notice that at the foot of each page in ELSA there is a space for further comment. This is provided for the teacher to make additional notes during the placement test. In particular it is supplied to enable the teacher to record further details of the pupil's performance on 'failed' objectives. This is important and needs some explanation.

The results recorded in the placement test column are quantative rather than qualitative.

For example, in H1 the pupil may have copied fourteen lower case letters accurately and made eight errors. This (quantitative) information tells you that the recommended criterion has not been achieved and that further teaching is required. But it does not tell you *which* letters can be copied satisfactorily and which need further attention.

Qualitative information of this kind is important when you start teaching. This additional data can save you a considerable amount of time during teaching. This issue is dealt with in detail in Chapter 5.

Carrying out the timed assessment involved in objectives which have a fluency criteria means that the child may not have opportunity to attempt all the items. Furthermore it is difficult in one minute or so for the teacher to keep detailed notes about the child's correct and incorrect responses. In this case we recommend that *after* the placement test you allow the child to attempt all (or most) of the items without any time constraint, whilst you make notes about his performance. As before, this information can then be recorded in the space at the foot of the page.

Using the placement test in the classroom

Having described in detail how any one of ELSA's teaching objectives can be assessed, we come to the question of how the placement test should be used in the classroom. For example, how do you decide which parts of ELSA to use with which children? And how can testing be fitted around normal classroom activities. Practical guidelines on some of these issues are provided below.

1. *Which children?*

It is assumed that you already know which children are most in need of extra help. Begin with just one pupil. As you become more familiar with the material you will be able to increase gradually the number of children working on ELSA.

How many children from a class of thirty you can eventually have working on parts of ELSA will depend upon a number of factors, not least your own organisational abilities. As a guide we can say that we have known many teachers, working alone in a class of thirty or more, who have been using one or more parts of ELSA with as many as six or seven pupils simultaneously. It should be emphasized however that this number was built up over a period of several weeks — always begin with just one pupil.

2. *Which subject areas?*

We assume that you already know not only which children need extra help but also in which subject areas the help is most needed. This will involve you in making priority decisions. Many children have difficulties in several aspects of the curriculum, but again we would recommend that you *begin with just one subject area*. Eventually, of course, you may have the same pupil working on three or four subject areas simultaneously. Alternatively you may be using one ELSA subject area but with several pupils.

3. *Which units?*

Choose whichever unit or units seem appropriate for each child. For example, if in Independence Skills you are concerned only about a pupil's difficulties in dressing, then assess the objectives in that unit and disregard the rest. Similarly, you may have a pupil who is making satisfactory progress through his reading scheme but would benefit (you think) from some additional phonic work. In such a case you could assess the objectives in the phonics units (i.e. units 3 and 4) but disregard units 1 and 2 in Reading.

By using your knowledge of your pupils to select different units for different children, you are not misusing ELSA. On the contrary — it was designed to be used flexibly and to allow teachers to select different parts for pupils according to individual needs.

For your guidance, however, the topsheet of each unit has a section called '*Entry Skills*'. As the name suggests, this is a brief description of what we recommend pupils should be able to do *before* tackling that particular unit. It is hoped that these notes will help you to decide which units to assess in the placement test with each pupil.

4. *Which teaching objectives?*

Assess *all the objectives* in any selected unit. This will vary from two to nine objectives according to the chosen unit.

The temptation to discontinue assessing objectives as soon as one is 'failed' should usually be resisted. In the next chapter we explain how to use placement test results to decide not only which objectives need further teaching but also the order in which they should be taught. To make these decisions you will need to know how well the pupil performed on *all* the objectives in any unit.

The implication of this recommendation is that you should assess even those objectives which you are fairly sure the pupil will fail. You need to know how far short of criteria the pupil performs and which aspects (if any) the pupil can perform satisfactorily. This suggestion must be interpreted *with discretion*. We are, in effect, suggesting that you deliberately expose the child to a certain amount of failure. To some extent this is inevitable in the process of determining the limits of the pupil's existing skills. Obviously you should discontinue work on any objective should there be signs of the pupil becoming distressed because of being asked to attempt a task which is clearly beyond him.

5. *Where and when to test?*

Ideally, testing should be carried out in a routine way in the pupil's normal classroom. This will probably mean arranging a few minutes occasionally when you can work individually with him at his desk. The total time necessary to assess a unit varies considerably, and depends upon the nature of the unit in question and the teacher's familiarity with the material. In some cases complete units can be assessed in five minutes. Some take rather longer, but none should take more than fifteen minutes.

Some teachers may be able to withdraw pupils from their normal class to work in a small group or even individually. In such circumstances testing could perhaps continue uninterrupted for twenty or even thirty minutes. There is no reason why ELSA should not be used in this way, and there are obvious advantages in terms of speeding up the assessment process. However, we would stress that ELSA was designed so that it *could* be used in the normal classroom and does not require 'clinical' conditions of this kind.

Final comment

The key issue with the primary school class teacher is invariably time! ELSA cannot create time, but it can help you use time more efficiently. We would make three final points in connection with the placement test which focus on the question of time:

1. Each part of the placement test need only be used once with each pupil. Thereafter the pupil records provide precise information about what each pupil can and cannot do.
2. All classteachers spend some time with individual pupils who are experiencing difficulties. All that is being suggested here is that — for a period — time is spent carrying out the replacement test. No more time need be found than you already use.
3. A great deal of time is wasted in many primary schools testing children — often (dare it be said) by headteachers, no less. The tests used often merely confirm that some children are better than others at various academic subjects, but provide no clue as to what might be done by the classteacher to help. The ELSA placement test takes time, but it provides information which is precise and tells you what to do next.

Self-test

The answers to the following questions are to be found at the end of the book, together with the number of the page on which the particular aspect is covered.

1. What are the three things to check before beginning an ELSA placement test with a pupil?
2. What, precisely, is the purpose of an ELSA placement test?
3. What are the four components of an ELSA teaching objective?
4. Where should the details of the pupil's placement test performance be recorded?
5. For each teaching objective assessed during a placement test you should record three pieces of information. What are they?
6. What information is provided to help you decide which units to assess in a placement test? Where can this be found?
7. What is the guideline for deciding which teaching objectives to assess in any unit?

Discussion points

1. ELSA assumes that the teacher has a reasonable knowledge of a child's strengths and weaknesses. How do teachers in your school collate this information and pass it on to colleagues?
2. Consider the contents of a selection of ELSA objectives, particularly the instructions to be used by the teacher and the recommended criteria. Do they seem appropriate for your pupils?
3. How do you establish performance criteria in your own teaching?
4. How does the time commitment involved in giving an ELSA placement test compare with other forms of assessment?
5. Describe a child with learning difficulties in your class and indicate which ELSA units would be most relevant to his needs.

Classroom assignment

Before reading Chapter 4, choose one child in your class and carry out a placement test using those units which seem to be most appropriate, given his existing attainments.

4

Choosing Objectives

To explain how placement test results are used to choose appropriate teaching objectives and decide the order in which they should be taught.

Having gathered detailed information about the pupil's existing attainments, your next step is to analyse this data in order to plan an individualised teaching programme. This will take the form of a sequence of objectives to be taught in a step-by-step manner.

Analysing the results

Often an experienced teacher will find that the teaching implications of the placement test results are quite obvious. They will usually show that:

1. Some objectives are already mastered, i.e. can be performed to the recommended criteria.
2. Some are partially acquired and need further attention, and
3. Others cannot yet be performed at all by the pupil.

Clearly those already mastered need no further teaching. Common-sense would dictate that teaching should commence on those items on which the pupil has already made a start. This can, however, be taken one step further in order to plan a more detailed teaching programme.

On the topsheet of each unit the teaching objectives are listed in an abbreviated form. The adjacent column is for recording your decisions about the order in which objectives should be taught. How, then, should this order be determined? This is an important professional decision that teachers must make in the light of the assessment they have carried out and the needs of the child concerned. Usually, however, the following guideline provides an acceptable solution:

> *Start work on the objective upon which the pupil is most likely to succeed,* i.e. the objective upon which the child seems nearest to the recommended criterion.

Similarly, the remaining objectives in the unit can then be listed according to the pupil's performance on each during the placement test. So, the ones he is nearest to achieving will come early in the list, whilst those upon which he performs less well will be left to the last.

We must stress that these are guidelines (and not rules) which should be interpreted thoughtfully. It may be, for example, that a particular objective, despite not being the obvious one to teach first from an analysis of the child's initial attempts, is so important as to take priority. In addition, you may well feel that a child can handle more than one objective at the same time.

In order to illustrate the issues involved in analysing placement test results we will consider two examples, the details of which appear in Figures 3 and 4.

The first example is taken from Unit 3 (Addition and Subtraction to 10) in ELSA Arithmetic. It can be seen that all three objectives were assessed on the same day, the whole placement test taking less than ten minutes. The child did not reach criteria on any of the items and an order of teaching had to be decided.

You will remember that the guideline is to start teaching on the objectives upon which the pupil is nearest to the recommended criteria. In this case this would be A9, on which the pupil made ten correct and three incorrect responses. After A9 would come A11, and finally A10 on which he had the least success. Thus the order of teaching was determined (i.e. A9 – A11 – A10) and recorded in the column provided.

The second example is taken from Unit 1 (Naming) in ELSA Language. It can be seen from Figure 4 that the unit was assessed on the 11th and 12th October (in two five-minute sessions), and that the recommended criterion (i.e. 10/10) was achieved on only one objective, i.e.

TEACHING OBJECTIVES:			PLACEMENT TEST RESULTS:	
			Date:	4th Oct.
A9	Adds two digits up to totals of 10 or less	1	√	×
			10	3
			Date:	4th Oct.
A10	Subtracts from 10 or less	3	√	×
			2	6
			Date:	4th Oct.
A11	Writes in missing numbers in addition sums to totals of 10 or less	2	√	×
			4	2

Figure 3: ELSA Arithmetic Unit 3: Addition and Subtraction to 10

TEACHING OBJECTIVES: / PLACEMENT TEST RESULTS:

	Teaching objective		Date	√	×
L1	Name ten body parts		11th Oct.	10	0
L2	Names ten more body parts	5	11th Oct.	4	6
L3	Names ten articles of clothing	3=	11th Oct.	8	2
L4	Names ten more articles of clothing from pictures	3=	12th Oct.	6	4
L5	Names ten classroom objects	1=	12th Oct.	9	1
L6	Names ten more classroom objects from pictures	1=	12th Oct.	8	2

Figure 4: ELSA Language Unit 1: Naming

L1. The pupil failed to reach criteria on the remaining five and an order of teaching these needed to be decided.

Using the presented guideline, L5 would be taught first followed by L3 *or* L6. However, as the pupil was so near to the recommended criteria on both L5 and L6 and because L5 and L6 both involve naming classroom objects it was decided to teach L5 and L6 simultaneously. On the same basis L3 and L4 were grouped to be taught next, and it was decided to teach L2 last. This second example shows how the guidelines should be interpreted flexibly and with discretion.

A note on criteria levels

With regard to all the criteria levels recommended in ELSA, some modification may be necessary for a few children. This should only be considered, however, in cases where pupils have sensory or physical handicaps which clearly have an effect on the quality of performance. For example, it may be necessary to reduce the fluency of oral responses required of a pupil with a speech impairment, or written responses where a child has a physical disability which impedes his hand movements.

On the other hand, it would not be legitimate to reduce the criterion for a reading objective simply on the grounds that a particular child is 'not very good at reading'. Classroom experience has shown that for most children the recommended criteria in ELSA are both realistic and advantageous.

If modifications to the recommended criteria levels are made for a child this should be noted on his record sheet.

Self-test

The answers to the following questions are to be found at the end of the book, together with the number of the page on which the particular aspect is covered.

1. Which teaching objectives can you assume need no further teaching or practice?
2. Under what circumstances might you decide to reduce, or in some other way change, the recommended criteria of any teaching objective?
3. What is the guideline for deciding which teaching objective should be taught first?
4. What is the guideline for deciding the teaching order of the remaining objectives?
5. Can you teach more than one objective at the same time?
6. Where should you record your decisions about the order in which you intend to work on objectives?

Discussion points

1. How do you plan individualised teaching programmes for pupils with special needs?
2. Consider the guidelines for determining the order in which objectives are to be taught. Do they seem appropriate?
3. Think of examples of where particular objectives might be regarded as a priority for a pupil.
4. Discuss the placement test results given in the two examples presented in the chapter.
5. Consider examples from your own experience where it might have been necessary to reduce criteria levels for a particular pupil.

Classroom assignment

Before reading Chapter 5, fill in the topsheets on the basis of the placement test which you have already carried out and determine an appropriate teaching order for the objectives.

5 Teaching to Objectives

To provide some practical suggestions about teaching to objectives

So far we have dealt with giving a placement test and using the results to design an individual programme of objectives for a pupil. In this chapter we look at some of the issues concerned with *teaching to objectives*. Although we cannot provide a step-by-step account of how each and every one of ELSA's teaching objectives should be taught, there are a number of issues of a more general nature which teachers will find helpful.

The chapter is divided into two parts. The first describes three phases of teaching and suggests ways in which this framework can be used to think about and plan the implementation of an ELSA teaching programme. The second part discusses other important practical issues concerning the use of ELSA in the classroom.

Three phases of teaching

In describing these three phases of teaching we must acknowledge the contribution of Norris Haring* and his colleagues at the University of Washington whose work has greatly influenced the ideas presented in this chapter. At the same time of course we would not wish to hold them responsible for our conclusions which in a number of respects do not correspond entirely with theirs.

The three phases of teaching are:

1. *Reducing errors*. Here the pupil is attempting a new skill and is inevitably making errors. The teacher's task is to reduce errors to a minimum.
2. *Increasing fluency*. Here the pupil can perform the skill independently, making very few errors. The teacher's task is now to increase his speed of response without sacrificing accuracy.
3. *Applying skills*. Here the pupil can perform the skill fluently. The teacher's task at this stage is to provide opportunities for the skill to be applied in a variety of settings using different materials and instructions.

These phases should not be seen as three discrete stages which have sharply defined boundaries. We cannot specify, for example, exactly how accurate a pupil must be on any particular ELSA objective before he should begin building fluency. Rather, the phases are presented as a framework for planning the use of an ELSA programme; they are provided as a rather crude but effective practical tool rather than a theory of learning!

In the next few pages the three phases of teaching are described in greater detail and their implications for planning the implementation of an ELSA teaching programme are discussed.

1. *Reducing errors*

When a pupil begins work on a new objective you should concentrate on his accuracy of response. This general rule holds whether the objective in question has an accuracy or a fluency criterion. During this phase the teacher's primary concern is to reduce errors to a minimum. The speed of response does not matter. In fact, to introduce a timed element into the proceedings here is tantamount to encouraging the pupil to perform a skill quickly which he cannot yet perform accurately — he would be practising errors.

We suggest in Chapter 3 that it is often helpful to make a note of the *actual* errors made in the placement test and not merely the number of errors. This information can save the teacher a great deal of time and help the pupil to reach criteria more quickly.

Often pupils can perform a number of parts or components of any 'failed' objective. For example, the child who failed L1 in the placement test may be able to name seven body parts and the child who failed R10 may be able to read aloud twenty short letter sounds. If, during the placement test, a note is taken of the actual errors made, the teacher knows even more precisely where to start teaching. In the examples above, it is likely that only three body parts and six letter sounds need intensive work.

This technique, known as 'teaching to errors', involves analysing placement test results even more carefully. The idea is to determine which parts or components of any failed objective have already been learnt and thus which parts need attention. Given the difficulties of finding time to give pupils individual attention, this is an important strategy for ensuring that available time is used most efficiently.

When using placement test data in this way it is important also to be aware that errors may develop on aspects of the ELSA objective which were performed successfully during the initial assessment. Remember therefore to have the pupil attempt the whole task from time to time. The tactics are the same. Identify and correct errors as they occur; do *not* let errors be practised and do *not* concern yourself at this stage with the pupil's speed of response.

It will be clear by now that during this 'reducing errors' phase a high degree of close supervision and individual attention is required. This is true, but we are not advocating any specialized or impractical arrangements — merely an efficient use of existing resources. Teachers, even those with the largest classes, teach children individually, not by taking them out of the classroom for long periods but by working with them at their desks for a few minutes when the class is busy. All that is being suggested here is that this time is spent to best effect during this

* Haring, N., and Eaton, M.D. (1978). Systematic Instruction Procedures: An Instructional Hierarchy. In Haring *et al.* (1978), *The Fourth R: Research in the Classroom*, Charles Merrill, Columbus, Ohio.

first teaching phase. This is the time when pupils need you most, and it will be seen that the demand for such close one-to-one attention is much reduced in the remaining two phases.

Finally, we said earlier that the three phases of teaching are not delineated by sharply defined cut-off points. Nevertheless, we can provide a rule of thumb for practical purposes. It is suggested that, usually, reducing errors should continue to be the main teaching strategy *until the pupil reaches the level of accuracy described in the objective's recommended criterion*. For ELSA objectives which have accuracy criteria this means teaching to errors until the pupil reaches the criteria, e.g. 5/5, 9/10. Remember that the pupil should be required to perform to criteria on two successive days.

For ELSA objectives which have fluency criteria this means teaching to errors until the standard of accuracy described in the recommended criteria has been achieved. In A9, for instance, fifteen correct and two errors is the *level* of accuracy required — irrespective of the time taken. In H4 twenty correct letters and two errors is the *level* of accuracy required — irrespective of the time taken. Remember too that this is a guideline and not a hard and fast rule.

2. *Increasing fluency*

Regrettably, many teachers do not plan their teaching in detail beyond the point where pupils are able to perform important skills accurately and independently. Frequently reaching this level of competence is a signal for the teacher to move on to a different and often more difficult aspect of the curriculum. Detailed planning, in other words, stops when acceptable accuracy levels are reached — with predictable consequences. The learnt skill simply decays. The pupil can no longer do what he could do quite well a few weeks earlier. Therefore, the second and third phases of teaching, although requiring much less one-to-one teaching, are as important as the first phase and should be just as carefully planned.

Building fluency involves increasing the pupil's speed of response without adversely effecting his level of accuracy. At this stage he is learning to perform skills more quickly which he can already perform accurately. This process obviously should not begin until the accuracy levels described earlier have been achieved.

The most obvious reason for requiring skills to be performed fluently is quite simply that pupils *need* to be able to work accurately and at speed in the classroom. The pupil, for example, who can copy from the blackboard accurately only if he works very slowly is liable to encounter all manner of problems. Reading slowly, taking too long to dress after PE, needing five minutes and a pile of bricks to add two single digits, and so on, are all likely to lead to difficulties. There are, however, other less obvious reasons for ensuring an adequate speed of response. These are that skills which can be performed fluently...

a. ... are less likely to be forgotten.
b. ... are more likely to be generalized to or applied in other important settings and contexts.
c. ... are more likely to facilitate the learning of more advanced skills.

It could be argued that, since we are emphasizing the importance of increasing fluency, all (and not just a proportion) of ELSA's objectives should have fluency criteria. Theoretically, there is indeed a strong case for measuring the time it takes for a pupil to dress, name body parts, spell words correctly, and so on. We have used fluency criteria *selectively* (i.e. in Reading, Arithmetic, and Handwriting only) because our experience suggests that this is the only realistic and practicable option available.

The implication of this compromise is that building fluency on objectives which have no fluency criteria is left to the professional judgement and common-sense of the class teacher. We assume that the pupil who has achieved an accuracy criterion will be provided with additional practice until the teacher is also satisfied with his speed of response. Clearly, there is no problem with ELSA objectives which have fluency criteria. These should be worked on until criterion is reached and the skill has been performed at this standard on two successive days.

Developing fluency necessitates far less teacher attention. At this level the pupil should be given plenty of opportunity for individual practice, including, where appropriate, exercises which involve repetition and drill. This means the development of interesting and attractive supplementary materials on which the child can work, perhaps using games or audio–visual materials to provide alternative forms of presentation.

Obviously at some point you will have to check the child's work, but this can usually be done after he has completed a section of work and should only take a few minutes. At this level also materials can frequently be developed which allow the pupil to check his own work.

With most children increasing the speed of response can be made into a game and usually has the effect of increasing interest and motivation. Games can be introduced which involve him in attempting to improve on his previous performance. For example, 'I know you can do these sums, but I want to see if you can get more right in five minutes than you did yesterday. Ready? ...' This idea is developed in Chapter 7 where more suggestions for increasing fluency are described.

3. *Applying skills*

In order to use ELSA objectives to best effect, teachers should be aware of their limitations as much as their strengths. Precise pupil objectives focus and concentrate the mind of teacher and pupil. Teaching and learning therefore become more clearly directed and purposeful. However, you should remember that the pupil who can perform a skill under particular conditions may not be able to perform the same skill under different circumstances. This applies to the pupil who has achieved the recommended criterion of one of ELSA's objectives.

Once a skill can be performed fluently the class teacher must ask: 'In what ways should the pupil be able to *apply* this skill?' The object of the exercise is to make sure that the skill described in the teaching objective can be generalized and adapted to other important classroom situations. With many children you cannot assume that this process will occur without your help.

Let us take an example from Unit 3 in ELSA Arithmetic. Objective A9 is concerned with adding two digits to totals of ten or less, A10 with subtracting from ten or less, and A11 involves writing in the missing numbers in addition sums to totals of ten or less. All three objectives have fluency criteria which we can assume have been achieved. In what ways should the pupil be able to apply these skills?

The materials for these objectives consist of horizontally presented sums, e.g. 3 + 6 = . The class teacher may decide that, in preparation for later ELSA objectives, the pupil should be able to perform these skills with vertically presented sums, e.g.

$$\begin{array}{llllllll} \text{(A9)} & 4 & \text{(A10)} & 5 & \text{(A11)} & & & 5 \\ & \underline{+1} & & \underline{-4} & & \underline{+3} & \text{or} & \underline{+} \\ & & & & & 7 & & 6 \end{array}$$

She could experiment with this unfamiliar format and find that most children can adapt to this change without difficulty. On the other hand, she may think that this is important enough to write a new objective, prepare appropriate materials, and describe a precise fluency criterion to which she and the pupil could aim.

Another important application of the skills in A9 and A10 concerns the question of printed or verbally presented problems which involve simple addition and subtraction. For example:

> There are 7 people on a bus. If 2 more get on how many people would be on the bus? (A9)
>
> John had 6 marbles. He lost 2. How many did he have left? (A10)

Remember that important applications of ELSA objectives may be built into later units. This is the case with Arithmetic where, in Unit 7, mixed addition and subtraction sums are presented.

Let us take one final example. Objectives L18 and L19 are concerned with spatial concepts like 'next to', 'under', and 'behind'. The pupil can achieve these objectives simply by responding appropriately to particular illustrations in the assessment material. You should not assume—even when the pupil can respond spontaneously and without error—that the same concepts can be understood and used appropriately in different situations. In this case the class teacher might contrive situations in the classroom or perhaps during PE to allow the skill to be practised in a wide range of different circumstances.

Opportunities for teaching the application of learnt skills may arise at any time and in any place. Teachers should be constantly looking out for suitable opportunities during normal class activities. This is often done informally and spontaneously as and when the opportunity occurs, but you may feel that it is necessary in certain situations to write some new objectives of your own to ensure that particularly important applications are made.

Figure 5 summarizes the three phases of teaching in table form. The remainder of this chapter looks at some other important aspects of using an ELSA programme in the classroom. Where appropriate these issues are related to the three phases.

Other practical issues

1. *Selecting teaching materials*

It is important that you make decisions about teaching materials *after* you have decided what you want the pupil to learn. Regrettably it sometimes happens that materials are chosen because they are bright and attractive, and then the teacher thinks about how they can be used. ELSA helps the teacher make more carefully considered decisions about materials since we have already determined what the pupil can already do and which objectives are to be taught next. Armed with this information the teacher can select materials which are specifically suited to particular teaching objectives.

Because high levels of performance are required before pupils are said to have achieved or mastered each objective, a child can sometimes be working on the same objective for quite a long time. The materials provided in the assessment material are sufficient merely to *assess* each teaching objective. Although they can obviously be used during teaching, in most cases they will be insufficient to sustain interest and motivation over an extended period.

When selecting or producing materials to supplement those provided, remember not to change the basic nature of the task. To use again the example from ELSA Arithmetic (i.e. A9 and A10), presenting addition sums in a vertical format or printed problems which involve single-digit addition and subtraction are *applications* of

PHASE	MAIN TEACHING METHODS	Until pupil ...
1. REDUCING ERRORS	(a) Teaching to errors made during placement test (b) Identifying and correcting other errors as they occur	Either (a) *Achieves the stated accuracy criterion,* e.g. points to own body parts in L1 (10/10) and L2 (10/10) or (b) *Achieves the standard of accuracy described in the fluency criterion,* e.g. reads aloud first 40 final 'e' words on Sheet R14 with 2 or less errors — irrespective of time taken
2. INCREASING FLUENCY	(a) Practise using supplementary (perhaps self-regulating) materials (b) Drill and repetition (c) Games 'against the clock' or 'beating your own previous score'	Either (a) *Performs objective which has no fluency criterion with a speed of response which is satisfactory to the teacher,* e.g. points to own body parts in L1 and L2 — spontaneously, i.e. without hesitation or (b) *Achieves the stated fluency criterion,* e.g. reads aloud final 'e' words on Sheet R14 at 40 per min with 2 or less errors
3. APPLYING SKILLS	(a) Practising learnt skills in unfamiliar settings as opportunities arise (b) Writing, and then teaching to, objectives which describe particularly important applications	*Applies skill in variety of situations to the satisfaction of the teacher.* Example 1. Names 20 body parts in L1 and L2 using (a) other children, (b) pictures of people Example 2. Reads words from R14 when mixed and presented with c–v–c words from R11

Figure 5: A Summary of the Three Phases of Teaching

the skill. It would be unwise therefore to introduce such materials until satisfactory fluency levels have been achieved, i.e. until the third (applying skills) phase of teaching. Until then supplementary materials should consist of sums in a horizontal format, perhaps (during the second phase) in the form of workcards with answers on the back for self-checking.

2. *Using praise and reward more effectively*

All teachers are aware of the importance of praising and rewarding pupils' achievements. Most are also aware that if only the most successful and capable pupils receive praise, there are some children who will miss out throughout their entire school career. Hence it is important to compare pupils with themselves rather than others, praising the less able for effort and progress which *for them* is good, even though what they have done may have been achieved by the rest of the class six months earlier.

One of the advantages of ELSA is that it will lead you to use praise more systematically, and therefore to greater effect. The placement test provides a baseline against which pupils' progress can be measured. It allows you to set clear objectives with precise criteria — a target at which you and the pupil can aim. You will inevitably begin to measure the pupil's progress towards the achievement of these objectives more carefully and you will spontaneously (and probably involuntarily) celebrate observable progress with praise. We have seen pupils and their teachers genuinely elated that an objective has been performed to criterion.

Children who experience difficulties in learning in several aspects of the curriculum and over a prolonged period often develop secondary, attitudinal problems. Such children may eventually become belligerent, pretend they do not care, say that learning is not important, and so on. In certain circumstances, therefore, it may be necessary to provide more tangible rewards for effort or for reaching criterion on a given objective. These might include house or credit points, a job around the school or in class which it is known the pupil enjoys, a trip to the headteacher, or a note home telling the parents that good progress is being made. The last of these suggestions is often very effective as it is so frequently the case in many schools that parents only receive letters when things are going badly.

What are the implications of the three phases of

teaching for the use of praise and reward? The most frequent praise is needed whilst reducing errors — during the first of the three phases. At this stage, the pupil needs comments and advice as he makes his attempts, immediate correction when he makes an error, and plenty of encouragement and praise for his successes. This underlines the need for concentrating individual attention during this phase of teaching. During the second and third phases, whilst the pupil is building fluency and learning to apply the skill in other situations, praise and reward can and should be provided on a much less frequent basis.

3. *Involving the pupil*

Teachers tend not to involve pupils sufficiently in making decisions about their own objectives. Indeed young, and particularly less able, pupils are often not even informed of these decisions after they have been made. As a result pupils are frequently set work without any explanation of what they are expected to learn, how good they are expected to get at it, or why it is important.

For example, it helps to explain the placement test and what it is intended to do. This does not mean that pupils need to read Chapter 3! Simply explain that you want to ... 'find out how well you can do some things .... Therefore, it is important you try very hard ...', etc.

It is also important that you take the time to explain to each pupil what his objective *is*. Admittedly this is not always easy and how it is done will depend on the nature of the objective and the pupil concerned. Nevertheless, given a little thought appropriate explanations can be provided — even with very young and sometimes quite seriously handicapped youngsters.

The main reason for stressing the importance of informing pupils of their own objective is that experimental evidence suggests that this actually facilitates learning. In other words, children are more likely to achieve their own objectives if they know what they are. How this operates is not fully understood, but a common-sense explanation is that children — like adults — are likely to work harder and more purposefully if they know what they are trying to achieve and why.

4. *Using available help in the classroom*

Despite the economic constraints of recent years some primary schools do have classroom helpers, a little of whose time you may be able to use to help the pupil with learning difficulties. Some schools use parent helpers and, even closer to hand, the assistance of older pupils can have a very positive effect, particularly where an older high-esteem pupil provides the help.

The contribution of these additional sources of help in the classroom can be made more effective and more directly linked to your teaching as a result of the existence of clearly stated teaching objectives. Moreover, the three phases of teaching described earlier provide a framework for planning the involvement of non-professionals.

We have already suggested that the class teacher's time is used to best effect during the first, 'reducing errors', phase of teaching. This is the time when the pupil needs immediate feedback on his performance and constant encouragement, and there are obvious dangers in devolving this responsibility to classroom helpers. The second and third phases — increasing fluency and applying skills — are less dependent on close, expert supervision but benefit greatly from the attention of an adult who understands the nature and purpose of the activity.

There follows a brief description of three kinds of activity which are related to the three phases and which can be usefully undertaken by non-professional help:

a. By recording the actual errors made during the placement test, the teacher can teach to the errors while the non-professional can be used to provide further practice and consolidation on those aspects of the objective which can be performed successfully. The class teacher's attention can be drawn to any particular errors should they emerge which cannot easily be corrected.
b. Fluency-building activities such as 'against-the-clock' and 'beat your previous score' games can be set up and supervized quite easily by helpers. Pupils can often spend quite some time in this second phase — perhaps they can tie shoelaces but not quickly enough, or read a passage from a book but not fluently enough. We have found that, once helpers understand the purpose of these activities, they can work in this way almost independently.
c. The application of skills which can already be performed fluently often needs planning by the class teacher but results in exercises and activities which can be undertaken by a non-professional. In all cases it is advisable to involve the helper by explaining the nature and purpose of the activity. This leads to a better understanding and ultimately to a more effective and meaningful contribution.

Some teachers who used ELSA in its pilot form organized the work of adult helpers using cards displayed on the classroom wall. Each pupil using ELSA had a card which was divided in half by a line. Above the line was a reminder to the class teacher of the objectives or their components on which the pupil was still making errors. Below the line were brief decriptions of activities suitable for either increasing fluency or applying skills. Helpers knew that, at certain times of the day, they could work individually with pupils who needed extra help. The cards enabled them to do this without constant reference to the class teacher and were renewed at fortnightly meetings to which classroom helpers were encouraged to attend.

5. *Involving parents*

Sometimes it seems that parents can't win! In some schools they are criticized for their apathy and lack of support and cooperation. And in others they are accused of being overanxious or of confusing the children by trying to teach them at home. There is mounting experimental evidence that parental involvement of the right kind can accelerate significantly the progress of youngsters with special needs. Moreover, it seems certain that there are many more parents who are willing to help in this way than many teachers believe.

Of course, there *are* parents who for whatever reason cannot be induced to work with their children at home, and it is true also that confusion can be generated by parents' anxiety that their children do well at school. However, this and earlier chapters have dwelt on the question of using time — the class teacher's most precious resource — more efficiently. Think of the time available to parents. If only they could be persuaded to use just some of that time to work constructively with their children.

One of the most difficult problems in this area is to get parents to compliment and support the school's efforts rather than work at cross purposes. The only way to achieve this is by communication. To this end ELSA can help. Parents can be involved in the use of ELSA teaching programmes in much the same ways as those described in the previous section on non-professional help. Most of these concern the consolidation and practice of skills already learnt at school. In other words, parental involvement can be focused on the second and third phases of teaching.

Two schools that have used parts of ELSA developed different ways of achieving this. Both invited parents to school initially to explain what was about to happen, but thereafter relied on written communications with periodic meetings to check on progress and problems. One of these schools, a nursery, simply sent home a postcard every ten to fourteen days describing skills recently learnt in school. The other involved parents in a spelling project by sending home a list of between three or six words each evening which had been taught that same day. In both cases the parents were being asked to consolidate and increase fluency, i.e. phase two activities. They were advised to spend no more than ten minutes each evening and to contact the school if there were any problems.

The two examples described above took very little time to organize, but two substantial benefits were derived. The children noticeably made more rapid progress and the parents greatly appreciated the opportunity to help.

Using ELSA should help you to provide parents with specific suggestions on how they can supplement and consolidate your work in school. Could you do more than you are at present doing to involve parents?

A final comment

Some teachers, on first learning about the objectives approach, comment that it seems rather cold and clinical. It is not difficult to understand how such an impression is formed. The approach can sound more technical and precise than other approaches in remedial and special education. It deals in criteria, precise assessment, and accurate pupil records, rather than emphasizing the importance of warmth, compassion, and understanding in the teacher's relationship with her pupils.

We have saved this point until last in the hope that it lingers in the memory of the reader. It is entirely irrational to assume that an approach that is systematic and efficient must also therefore be cold and depersonalized. Quite the contrary; ELSA requires a positive and warm relationship between teacher and pupil, and ELSA makes it easier for such relationships to be developed. Above all else ELSA enables the teacher to teach, to set work, and provide practice in ways which are accurately matched to the needs of the individual pupil at any given time. This is the key to developing self-confidence and a positive attitude to learning.

Self-test

The answers to the following questions are to be found at the end of the book, together with the number of the page on which the particular aspect is covered.

1. What are the three phases of teaching?
2. On what should you concentrate when a child begins work on a new objective?
3. In the context of using ELSA what does 'teaching to errors' involve?
4. What does the child need during the 'reducing errors' phase?
5. What is the pupil doing at the stage of 'increasing fluency'?
6. What is the purpose of the 'applying skills' phase?
7. Why are the assessment materials provided in ELSA insufficient?
8. How does ELSA help you praise and reward more effectively?
9. How can the contribution of parents and classroom helpers be linked to your own teaching with ELSA?
10. Why is it a good idea to let your pupils know their own teaching objectives?

Discussion points

1. How can time be found in a busy classroom to provide pupils with individual attention?
2. What teaching materials should be used to develop fluency?
3. Think of examples of how previously learnt skills might be applied in a variety of settings.
4. Do you feel that you use praise and reward effectively with your children?
5. Consider ways in which parents and other adults might be used to help a child achieve his objectives.

Classroom assignment

Before reading Chapter 6, plan and implement appropriate teaching methods for the individual programme of objectives you have devised. In particular consider ways of increasing fluency and applying skills.

6

Recording Pupils' Progress

Chapter Goal

To explain the use of ELSA for keeping records and to describe how these procedures fit into current ideas about assessment

By now you have given a placement test and used the results to design an individual programme of objectives for a pupil, and considered some of the issues involved in teaching to objectives. Without doubt one of the most important benefits of ELSA is that it provides an efficient method of keeping accurate pupil records.

This chapter has two parts. In the first is a brief description of how ELSA records should be used in the classroom and in the second is a discussion of how these procedures and their inherent advantages fit into current ideas about assessment.

Keeping the records

We suggest in Chapter 3 that any unit in the placement test need only be administered once with any pupil. If the records are kept up to date you will know at any time what the child can do, what he is currently working on, and what has yet to be started. Moreover, you will know how long it takes the pupil to master each objective, and you will have a reminder that previously mastered objectives need to be checked systematically to ensure that learnt skills are not forgotten. You will have all of this merely by writing the date in a box every now and again.

On each of the pages of ELSA there are three columns on the extreme right-hand side headed 'working on', 'mastered', and 'checked'. The essence of the record keeping system is that the teacher enters dates into the columns opposite the appropriate teaching objectives.

The procedure is as follows:

1. When work on a new objective is commenced, write the date in the *working on* column.
2. When the objective is mastered (i.e. when the pupil can perform the skill to the recommended criterion), write the date in the *mastered* column. Remember that the pupil should perform to criteria on two successive days before you record that the objective has been mastered. Use the date of the second of the two days.
3. Two or three weeks after the pupil has mastered an objective check that it can still be performed to the recommended criterion. If it is, then record that date in the *checked* column. If it is not, then provide further practice until the criterion is reestablished and record that date in the checked column.

The procedure outlined above is quick and accurate. It involves no more time than is required to enter a date into a column whenever work is commenced on an objective, or an objective is either mastered or checked. It is so quick in fact that entries can be made in the classroom when it happens.

Two further points should be made about this system of record keeping. In Chapter 5 we discuss the need to explain simply to pupils what they are working on and why and how good they are expected to get at it. The keeping of records can also be made to involve the pupil directly. On the simplest level the pupil can watch you date the mastered column whilst you explain how well he has done, how pleased the headteacher will be, and so on. Some teachers go one step further and use wall charts to display progress. This can be done by adding a star, a smiley face (or whatever) to a chart each time an objective is mastered. This kind of visual display of progress acts as a potent incentive to many children.

Record keeping and assessment

The word 'assessment' continues to be misunderstood by a great many teachers. To many, still, it has connotations of psychologists, remedial experts, restricted tests, and technical reports. Assessment to many remains the province of the expert — it does not involve the class teacher and it hardly ever occurs in the classroom. In recent years the word 'assessment' has been redefined. Assessment and record keeping are considered to be synonymous. Record keeping *is* assessment.

There are many reasons for this redefinition, but basically it is because it is now widely accepted that the most relevant information a teacher can have is information about what the learner already knows. If you do not know this, you do not know where to start teaching. Assessment therefore needs to be continuous — because what the pupil knows changes (literally) from one day to the next. It needs to be carried out in the classroom and by the class teacher — because the teacher is the only professional who sees the pupil frequently.

Using ELSA to keep records of pupil progress, ASSESSMENT becomes ...

1. ... *the responsibility of the class teacher*. By using ELSA, assessment becomes an integral part of your teaching. It is continuous and is carried out in the classroom.
2. ... *accurate*. ELSA consists of precise teaching objectives. Your records indicate when each pupil began work on an objective or mastered an objective to a recommended criterion. They are an accurate record of your classroom observations. They do not need to be interpreted and are therefore not open to misinterpretation.
3. ... *meaningful*. The ELSA records do not contain jargon. They can be understood by teachers (for example) in team teaching situations and, with a little explanation, classroom assistants, parents, and even pupils. Moreover, there is no reason why such records should be confidential — they can be used as a basis for reports to parents and, if necessary, other professionals.

4. ... *prescriptive*. Pupil records in some schools contain a lot of information which is of little use to anyone, but do not contain information which the teacher needs to decide what to do next. The ELSA records tell you what needs further practice, what should be taught next, and what needs to be checked. ELSA contains no superfluous or redundant information.
5. ... *a safeguard against prolonged exposure to failure*. The placement test reduces the likelihood of any pupil being given work which is much too difficult. By dating the 'working on' column you have a built-in early-warning system should the pupil fail to make satisfactory progress.
6. ... *a means of comparing a pupil's current and previous attainments*. Norm-referenced tests provide a standardized score which tells you how one pupil compares with other children of a similar age. Reading ages and IQ scores are norm-referenced. The ELSA records, on the other hand, are criterion referenced and provide the more useful comparison between one pupil's current and previous attainments.
7. ... *a safeguard against learnt skills being forgotten*. The 'checked' column ensures that learnt skills are checked systematically two or three weeks after the recommended criterion has been reached. Although this does not entirely resolve a particularly difficult problem, it represents a considerable improvement on a great deal of current practice.
8. ... *quick and easy to maintain*. The above benefits are enjoyed as a result of merely writing dates into three columns.

Self-test

The answers to the following questions are to be found at the end of the book, together with the number of the page on which the particular aspect is covered.

1. What will you know about a child if his ELSA records are kept up to date?
2. Why should previously mastered objectives be checked systematically?
3. In addition to the space for placement test results, the ELSA records have three columns. What are they?
4. What should be written in these three columns?
5. What is the most relevant assessment information a teacher can have?
6. How often should assessment be carried out when using ELSA?

Discussion points

1. What are the advantages of using dates when keeping records?
2. Is it necessary to check that all objectives can still be performed two or three weeks after they have been mastered?
3. How does the ELSA record-keeping procedure compare with others used in schools?
4. What are the main advantages of teachers taking responsibility for assessment? Are there any disadvantages?
5. How do you feel about allowing pupils or parents to see the records?

Classroom assignment

Use the ELSA records to monitor the progress of the child through your programme of objectives. Do not forget to go back occasionally and check on previously mastered items. If he is not making satisfactory progress you might consider the two advanced techniques described in Chapter 7.

7

Advanced Techniques

Chapter Goals

1. To describe how ELSA teaching objectives can be *task-analysed* to produce more finely graded teaching programmes
2. To describe how techniques of *daily measurement* can be incorporated into the use of ELSA

Chapters 3 to 6 describe how ELSA should be used in the classroom to:

1. Find out what a pupil can and cannot do.
2. Choose and sequence teaching objectives.
3. Plan teaching strategies.
4. Keep accurate records of pupil progress.

For many class teachers with large classes who have no regular adult help, using even parts of ELSA in this way with only a few pupils requires a lot of extra work and good classroom organization. It is possible therefore that many of the ideas presented in this chapter will be of little more than academic interest to some readers. The extent to which they can be used in practice depends obviously on the setting — the class size, the amount of adult help available, and so on.

In Chapter 5 three phases of teaching are described, i.e. reducing errors, increasing fluency, and applying skills. The two advanced techniques described in this chapter — task analysis and daily measurement — relate to the first two of these three phases:

a. *Task analysis*. We describe in Chapter 4 how ELSA objectives can be selected and sequenced for the individual pupil on the basis of placement test results. Some children, however, need more detailed, finely graded programmes which have much smaller steps. Task analysis consists of a range of methods for 'breaking down' teaching objectives. It is concerned therefore with the first phase of teaching — *reducing errors*.

b. *Daily measurement*. We describe in Chapter 6 how, by dating the three columns, ELSA can be used to keep records of pupil progress. Such records are probably more detailed and accurate than those used in most schools. However, it is possible and sometimes desirable to keep even more detailed records. This involves the daily measurement of pupils' progress towards the achievement of objectives which have fluency criteria. It therefore concerns the second of the two phases — *increasing fluency*.

The remainder of this chapter describes in detail how these two techniques can be applied to the use of ELSA in the classroom.

A. TASK ANALYSIS

When pupils start work on an objective they can often already perform several components of it. For example, the pupil working on A10 may be able to subtract from seven and below quite reliably, and make errors only when subtracting from eight, nine or ten. Similarly, the pupil starting work on H1 may already be able to copy accurately twenty-one of the lower case letters and have difficulty only with the other five. In both cases you would 'teach to the errors', as described in Chapter 5 — a detailed task analysis is unnecessary.

It is appropriate therefore to consider task-analysing ELSA objectives only if the pupil's initial performance on that objective falls well below the recommended criteria. If, in A10 for example, the pupil could not subtract from even three or four without making errors then a task analysis would be helpful. Similarly, if in H1 the pupil could copy only five or six letters to your satisfaction, then this too might be broken down. As a general rule, therefore:

> *The nearer to the recommended criteria a pupil is when you start work on an objective, the less likely you are to need a task analysis.*

This is an important practical point. The methods of task analysis outlined in the following pages can be used to generate programmes with ten or even more steps. Before producing and using such a programme, think carefully! Does the pupil need a finely graded step-by-step approach? Or would he reach the standard required in the objective quicker simply by concentrating on the errors made in the placement test?

An objective need usually be task-analysed only once. If you break down an objective for one pupil, it will almost certainly be useful with others. Over a period of time, therefore, you can build up a stock of finely graded teaching programmes consisting of task-analysed ELSA objectives. If more than one teacher is using ELSA in a school, obviously such programmes can be pooled — the work is thus shared and time is saved. Better still, if this text is used as a basis for in-service workshops, a resource bank of finely graded programmes can very quickly be accumulated by having groups of teachers task-analyse objectives from different subject areas.

There are several forms of task analysis, but the one which is most widely applicable to ELSA is *slicing*. This is described in detail in the following section with several worked examples taken from different subject areas. There are also

ELSA Pupil: ____________________

L2	None	Pointing to body parts (i.e, teeth, knee cheek, wrist, toe, hair, neck, ankle, Shoulder, elbow.). 'What's this?'	Names ten more body parts.	10/10

Code	STEPS TO OBJECTIVE L2	Records: Working on	Mastered	Checked
L 2.01	Names 'teeth', 'knee', and 'cheek' on request. (3/3).			
L 2.02	Names 'wrist', 'toe', and 'hair' on request. (3/3)			
L 2.03	Names the body parts in L.2.01 and L 2.02 on request. (6/6)			
L 2.04	Names 'neck', 'elbow', 'shoulder', and 'ankle' on request. (4/4)			

Figure 6

ELSA Pupil: ____________________

L2	None	Pointing to body parts (ie. teeth, knee, cheek. wrist, toe, hair, neck, ankle, shoulder, elbow.) 'What's this?'	Names ten more body parts.	10/10

Code	STEPS TO OBJECTIVE L2	Records: Working on	Mastered	Checked
L 2.01.	Names 'teeth' and 'knee' on request. (2/2)			
L 2.02	Names 'cheek' and 'wrist' on request. (2/2)			
L 2.03	Names body parts in L 2.01 and L 2.02 on request. (4/4)			
L 2.04	Names 'toe' and 'hair' on request. (2/2)			
L 2.05	Names 'neck' and 'elbow' on request. (2/2)			
L 2.06	Names body parts in L.2.04 and L.2.05 on request. (4/4)			
L 2.07	Names 'Shoulder' and 'ankle' on request. (2/2)			

Figure 7

a number of other approaches to task analysis which are less simple and less widely applicable to ELSA. Some of these are described in rather less detail in a later section.

Slicing

This method of task analysis, which can be used with most of the objectives in ELSA, is very simple. Indeed, teachers have been using the technique for many years without giving it this name. It is merely a way of breaking down an objective into smaller, more manageable 'bits'. The teacher wanting to teach a pupil twenty-six letter sounds, for example, would not teach them all at once. She would split the letters into smaller groups of perhaps five or six letters, and teach one group at a time. This is slicing.

Let us take another example. Objective L2 — 'Names ten more body parts' — can be sliced. Obviously, this would involve teaching a smaller number of body parts at each step in the programme until all ten have been taught. In writing the programme, however, there are two important decisions to be made:

1. How small should the steps be?
2. How many revision steps should there be?

The answers to both of these questions depend upon the pupil, or group of pupils, for whom the programme is intended.

Look at Figures 6 and 7. Both programmes lead to the same objective, L2. In the first, the ten body parts are taught in groups of three (L2.01), three (L2.02), and four (L2.04). A revision item is inserted (L2.03) so that the six body parts taught up to that point are consolidated before teaching the remaining four.

In the example in Figure 7 the ten body parts are taught in five pairs (L2.01, L2.02, L2.04, L2.05, and L2.07) and revision items are inserted at L2.03 and L2.06. Hence there are four steps in the first programme and seven steps in the second. In this way the number of steps in the programme and the number of revision steps can be matched to the needs of the particular pupil or pupils for whom it is intended.

You will notice that in the two examples provided the steps in the programme have been coded. We have found this to be a useful convention, especially in schools where a number of such programmes have been produced and need to be stored and retrieved for easy reference. The letter and number on the left of the decimal point corresponds to the original ELSA code and the number on the right indicates the teaching order. L2.01 is written thus (as opposed to L2.1) because some programmes may have more than ten steps in which L2.1 would need to be distinguished from L2.10.

You will notice too that the four-column format has not been used in the task analysis. Because the basic nature of the task being presented to the pupil is not different to the ELSA objective, an abbreviated form can be used without losing any important information. We suggest that each step in the programme should be performed to the criterion specified in brackets on two successive days before moving on to the next step. The record keeping system is the same as that presented in Chapter 2. A blank form which can be reproduced to write your own programmes is provided on the next page.

With the example from ELSA Language the ten body parts could be sliced in any way you wish. That is, there is no reason why body parts should be grouped together in any particular way to form steps. This is not always the case. Look at the programme in Figure 8 'Reads aloud consonant–vowel–consonant words'. Slicing has again been used. However, instead of randomly subdividing the sixty words in R11, the slicing has been carried out according to the medial vowel of the word. That is to say, the twelve words with a medial 'a' are taught in R11.01, the words with a medial 'e' in R11.02, and so on. Revision steps have been inserted at R11.03 and R11.06. A finer breakdown involving a total of fifteen steps could be produced by teaching only six words at each step and inserting a revision item after every twelve words.

When task-analysing an ELSA objective using slicing you should always look for a logical way of breaking down the task. All of the objectives in Unit 4 of ELSA Reading, for example, can be sliced logically, according to the medial vowel, consonant blend, or letter combination in the words. (A further example is provided in Figure 9.) If there is no obvious logical basis for slicing, then the objective must be broken down into smaller teaching steps randomly.

There is another important difference between L2 and R11. The recommended criterion for the latter — unlike the former — is described as a measure of fluency (i.e. 40 per min, Max. 2 errors). We would suggest that when task-analysing objectives which have fluency criteria the steps should focus on the *accuracy* of the pupil's response and *not* the speed. At this stage the pupil is in the process of reducing errors and it is only important that he learns to perform the skill accurately. Building fluency should be left until the programme has been completed. You will notice therefore that the criteria specified in brackets at each step impose no constraints on the speed of response.

A final point can be noted in connection with R11. In order to make this programme easier to use in the classroom additional materials should be prepared. You will need seven word lists — one for each of the steps in the programme. The alternative to producing this material is to use sheet R11 on page 189, but this would involve searching for the words with a particular medial vowel which are scattered randomly across the

ELSA Pupil: ____________________

R11	Sixty different C-V-C words with each vowel used 12 times. Present for 1 minute.	'Read these words quickely, trying not to make mistakes'	Reads aloud Consonant-vowel-Consonant words.	40 per min Max: 2 errors.

Code	STEPS TO OBJECTIVE R11	Records: Working on	Mast-ered	Checked
R 11.01	Reads aloud consonant-short 'a'-consonant (11/12)			
R 11.02	Reads aloud consonant-Short 'e'-Consonant words, eg. red. (11/12)			
R. 11.03	Reads aloud words in R.11.01 and R.11.02 (21/24).			
R 11.04	Reads aloud consonant-Short 'i'-Consonant words, eg. pig. (11/12)			
R 11.05	Reads aloud consonant-Short 'o'-Consonant words, eg. dog. (11/12)			
R. 11.06	Reads aloud words in R.11.04 and R.11.05 (21/24)			
R. 11.07	Reads aloud consonant-short 'u'-Consonant words, e.g. but. (11/12)			

Figure 8.

ELSA Pupil: ____________________

R 15	Sixty words with Combinations ai, ng, th, sh, ea, and ur. Presented for 1 minute.	'Read these words quickly trying not to make mistakes'.	Reads aloud words with letter Combinations.	40 per min. Max: 2 errors.

Code	STEPS TO OBJECTIVE R.15	Records: Working on	Mast-ered	Checked
R. 15.01	Reads aloud words with 'sh' Combinations e.g. shed. (9/10)			
R 15.02	Reads aloud words with 'ng' combinations, e.g. ring (9/10)			
R 15.03	Reads aloud words in R.15.01 and R 15.02. (18/20)			
R 15.04	Reads aloud words with 'ea' Combination. e.g. seat (11/12)			
R 15.05	Reads aloud words with 'ur' Combination, e.g. hurt (7/8)			
R 15.06	Reads aloud words in R 15.04 and R 15.05. (18/20)			
R 15.07	Reads aloud words with 'ai' Combination, eg. paid (11/12)			
R 15.08	Reads aloud words with 'th' Combination, eg. bath (7/8)			
R 15.09	Reads aloud words in R 15.07 and R 15.08. (18/20)			

Figure 9

ELSA

Pupil: ____________________

Code	STEPS TO OBJECTIVE	Records		
		Working on	Mast-ered	Checked

page. Thus, for example, the word lists needed for R11.01 to R11.03 would be:

R11.01: cat bat van pal fat can jam dad bag tap bad man
R11.02: red bed pen jet ten men let yes pet leg get wet
R11.03: wet red can jam pet jet van tap men bat fat get leg bed yes pen cat dad ten bag bad let

Let us take one final example of an objective which has been sliced logically. Look at the programme in Figure 10 and a sample of the materials required in Figure 11. You will notice that the slicing has been carried out on the basis of the *totals* of the addition sums, i.e. the sum of the two digits gradually increases through the programme. Again, although A9 has a fluency criterion, the standard of performance required at each step in the programme focuses on the accuracy of the pupil's response and fluency building is deferred until the programme has been completed.

The above description of the use of slicing should be sufficient to enable you to apply the technique to the task analysis of other ELSA objectives. In the following section a number of other techniques of task analysis are presented.

Other methods

Although the methods of task analysis described in this section have been used extensively in the development of curriculum material for severely handicapped children, they are not at present in widespread use in primary schools. Nevertheless, their potential is considerable, particularly in nursery and reception classes where there is a curriculum bias towards self-help skills, gross

ELSA Pupil: ____________________

A9	Thirty different addition sums totalling 10 or less. Presented for 1 minute.	'Do these sums as quickley as you can trying not to make any mistakes.'	Adds two digits up to totals of 10 or less (written response).	15 per min Max. 1 error

Code	STEPS TO OBJECTIVE A9	Records		
		Working on	Mastered	Checked
A 9.01	Adds 2 digits to totals of 4 or less (9/10)			
A 9.02	Adds 2 digits to totals of 5 or 6. (9/10)			
A 9.03	Adds 2 digits to totals of 6 or less. (9/10).			
A 9.04	Adds 2 digits to totals of 7 or 8. (9/10)			
A 9.05	Adds 2 digits to totals of 8 or less (9/10).			
A 9.06	Adds 2 digits to totals of 9 or 10 (9/10).			

Figure 10

A9.01

0 + 4 =	1 + 1 =	3 + 1 =
1 + 2 =	3 + 0 =	0 + 1 =
1 + 0 =	2 + 2 =	0 + 2 =
1 + 3 =	4 + 0 =	0 + 0 =
2 + 1 =	0 + 3 =	2 + 0 =

A9.02

5 + 0 =	1 + 5 =	4 + 1 =
1 + 4 =	6 + 0 =	2 + 4 =
4 + 2 =	0 + 5 =	3 + 3 =
3 + 2 =	3 + 3 =	0 + 6 =
5 + 1 =	2 + 3 =	4 + 1 =

Figure 11

and fine motor skills, and simple discrimination tasks.

We must stress that the brief descriptions provided here are introductory; they may not be sufficiently detailed to enable you to generalize these methods to the task analysis of other ELSA objectives.

If you intend to use these methods extensively to produce a number of teaching programmes, we would recommened that you contact your local educational psychologist or special education adviser who should be able to advise on their use in the development of finely graded teaching programmes.

Four methods of task analysis are described in this section:

1. Chaining
2. Shaping
3. Errorless discrimination learning
4. Fading

These do *not* represent the sum total of available techniques. Indeed, some of ELSA's teaching objectives can only be task-analysed in ways not described here, and some require a combination of more than one method of task-analysis.

1. *Chaining*

Chaining can be used when the skill to be taught consists of a number of components *each of which can be performed independently*. It involves identifying the components, and 'linking' or 'chaining' them together in the desired order of performance. Examples of skills which can be taught in this way include putting on and removing articles of clothing and washing and drying hands. The latter, for instance, can be broken down into several components — putting in the plug, rolling up sleeves, filling the basin, using soap, rinsing hands, emptying the basin, etc. Because each of these components can be performed independently, the objective 'washing and drying hands' may be taught by 'chaining' the components in the desired order.

For some skills *forward* chaining can be used. This involves teaching the first component in the temporal sequence first. Once this step has been achieved, the first and second components are taught; then the first, second, and third components; and so on until the objective has been mastered.

A more widely applicable technique is *backward* chaining. The skill of putting on a pair of socks is taught using backward chaining in Figure 12. Here the last component in the temporal sequence is taught first, then the last and second last, and so on. The major benefit of backward chaining is that at each step in the programme the pupil completes the task successfully. As a rule, this is more rewarding for the pupil than having the teacher finish off the task — which is usually necessary with forward chaining.

As suggested earlier, sometimes more than one method of task analysis is used to produce a programme. Look at the example in Figure 13. Here the pupil is taught to count to five (i.e. A1.04) and then to ten (i.e. A1.09). This is *forward* chaining. But then these two steps have been *backward*-chained: up to five in A1.01 to A1.04 and up to ten in A1.05 to A1.09.

2. *Shaping*

Some skills, particularly those which involve fine motor coordination, can be task-analysed using shaping. In such a programme the pupil is expected to perform the same skill throughout, but specially prepared teaching materials are carefully graded — from larger-than-life models, in successive approximations, to life size.

Look at the example in Figure 14. Here two things are happening. First, the task of doing up buttons is being taught on hand-held materials and, second, the size of the buttons and buttonholes is being gradually reduced from I5.01 to I5.04. This is shaping. It is a technique which can be used with a few of ELSA's objectives, such as tying up and untying shoelaces.

The equipment required to use this and similar programmes are time-consuming to produce and obviously the class teacher will need to decide whether the time and effort required is

ELSA Pupil: ____________________

from I/	Socks (off)	'Put on your socks'	Puts on socks.	2/2

Code	STEPS TO OBJECTIVE from I/	Records: Working on	Mast-ered	Checked
I 1.01	Pulls up socks from ankles. (2/2)			
I 1.02	Pulls up socks from heels (2/2)			
I 1.03	Pulls up socks from insteps (2/2)			
I 1.04	Pulls up socks from toes (2/2)			

Figure 12

ELSA Pupil: ____________________

A1	None	'Count up to 10'.	Counts aloud to 10	10/10

Code	STEPS TO OBJECTIVE A1	Records: Working on	Mast-ered	Checked
A 1.01	'Count up to 5 with me ... 1, 2, 3, 4, —' (1/1)			
A 1.02	'Count up to 5 with me ... 1, 2, 3 — . — .' (2/2)			
A 1.03	'Count up to 5 with me .... 1, 2, —. —. —.' (3/3)			
A 1.04	'Count up to 5 with me ... 1, —. —. —. —' (4/4)			
A 1.05	'Count up to 10 with me ... 1, —. —. —. —. 6. 7. 8. 9. —' (5/5)			
A 1.06	'Count up to 10 with me .... 1, —, —. —. —, 6, 7. 8, —, —' (6/6)			
A 1.07	'Count up to 10 with me .... 1, —. —. —. —. 6, 7, —. —. —' (7/7)			
A 1.08	'Count up to 10 with me ... 1, —, —. —. —. 6, —. —. —. —' (8/8)			
A 1.09	'Count up to 10 with me ... 1, —. —. —. —. —. —. —. —. —' (9/9)			

Figure 13

ELSA Pupil: ______________

from — I5	Garment (ON) with four accessible buttons.	'Do up your buttons'.	Does up four buttons	4/4

Code	STEPS TO OBJECTIVE (from I5)	Records: Working on	Mast-ered	Checked
I 5.01	Does up four 1-in diameter buttons in held garment or material. (4/4)			
I 5.02	Does up four 3/4-in diameter buttons in held garment or material. (4/4)			
I 5.03	Does up four 1/2-in diameter buttons in held garment or material. (4/4)			
I 5.04	Does up four dress or shirt buttons in held garment or material. (4/4)			

Figure 14

ELSA Pupil: ______________

from — L15	Pictures of five shapes; (□, ○, ▭, △, and ◇.)	'Show me the triangle.'	Points to triangle	5/5

Code	STEPS TO OBJECTIVE (from L15)	Records: Working on	Mast-ered	Checked
L 15.01	Present △: 'Show me the triangle.' (5/5)			
L 15.02	Present △, ▭ in either order: 'Show me the triangle.' (5/5)			
L 15.03	Present △, ▭, ○ in either order: 'Show me the triangle.' (5/5)			
L 15.04	Present △, ▭, □, ○ in any order: 'Show me the triangle.' (5/5)			
L 15.05	Present ○, ▭, □, △, ◇ in any order: 'Show me the triangle.' (5/5)			
	REPEAT SEQUENCE FOR EACH SHAPE.			

Figure 15

ELSA Pupil: ____________________

from M9	Picture of Square. Presented twice. Paper and pencil.	'Copy this shape'.	Copies Square.	2/2

Code	STEPS TO OBJECTIVE from: M9.	Records		
		Working on	Mast-ered	Checked
M 9.01	Copies square from modal-given squares with broken lines. (3/3)			
M 9.02	Copies square from modal-given squares with reduced prompts. (3/3)			
M 9.03	Copies square from modal-given four angled corners. (3/3)			
M 9.04	Copies square from modal-given four dotted corners. (3/3)			

Figure 16

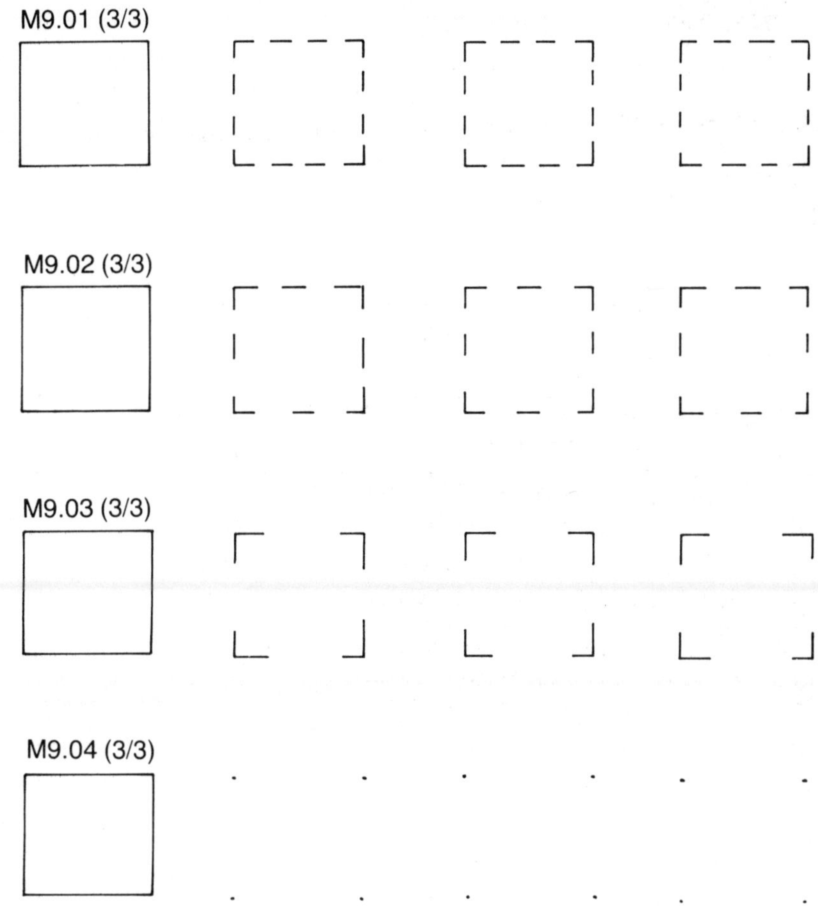

Figure 17

justified in terms of the frequency with which such materials would be used.

3. *Errorless discrimination learning (EDL)*

EDL can be used to task-analyse ELSA objectives which involve the pupil making discriminations (for example) between shapes or colours. Look at the example in Figure 15. ELSA objective L15 requires the pupil to state the name of the five shapes. Most teachers would first teach the simpler skill of pointing to a shape when it is asked for by name, teaching only one shape at a time.

This programme illustrates the two essential elements of an EDL task analysis. First, *the number of items to pick from* (i.e. the choice array) *is gradually increased* throughout the programme. In L15.01 the pupil is pointing to a circle when he has nothing else to point to, but by step L15.05 he is pointing to a circle when presented with five different shapes. Second, the 'power' of the 'distractors' is gradually increased throughout the programme. That is to say, the shapes which the pupil is most likely to confuse are introduced in the later steps of the programme so that he is making discriminations between grossly dissimilar shapes in the earlier steps. In this case, for example, the diamond is introduced into the array last of all as it is probably the shape most likely to be confused with a triangle.

4. *Fading*

Fading is a method of task analysis which involves the gradual reduction of prompts and cues. The technique is used extensively in the teaching of a wide range of skills with mentally handicapped children. However, it has been applied to paper and pencil tasks in normal schools with considerable success. Look at the example in Figure 16 and the sample material associated with the programme (Figure 17). At each step in the programme the amount of help given to the pupil is reduced simply by reducing the visual prompts provided.

Fading can be applied in this way to the ELSA objectives which are concerned with forming letters and numerals (i.e. H1, H2, and H3) and all the shapes in M9 from which the example is taken.

Final comment

For most of the time, detailed step-by-step teaching programmes of the kind described in this chapter are *not* necessary for most pupils. Such programmes should only be used in situations where the pupil is nowhere near achieving the ELSA objective in question.

If you do need a more finely graded programme think first about slicing since, of the range of techniques of task analysis described in this chapter, it is the most widely applicable. When using this approach, remember:

1. Try to match the 'step size' and the number of revision steps to the needs of the pupil for whom the programme is intended.
2. Study the objective carefully for a logical way of breaking down the task, e.g. by the medial vowel.
3. Use only accuracy criteria in the steps of the programme — even if the ELSA objective itself has a fluency criterion.
4. When using the programme have the pupil perform each step to the specified criteria on two successive days before moving on to the next step.
5. Prepare additional materials as they are needed to make the programme easier to use in the classrooom.

Chaining, shaping, errorless discrimination learning and fading are four other techniques of task analysis which can be used with a number of ELSA objectives. Readers who wish to pursue these approaches are recommended to refer to:

Gardner, J., Murphy, J., and Crawford, N. (1983). *The Skills Analysis Model*, British Institute of Mental Handicap, Kidderminster.

B. DAILY MEASUREMENT

Most of ELSA's teaching objectives can be assessed with an individual pupil in one or two minutes. Daily measurement means simply that an objective is assessed every day and the pupil's daily performance is marked on a chart. Hence you are measuring a pupil's daily progress towards the achievement of a particular objective. In other words, daily measurement is a sophisticated form of record keeping, more detailed than the procedures described previously, which focuses on what is happening between the dates when a pupil starts work on, and finally masters, an objective.

Before describing when and how this technique can be used with the ELSA material it should be said that the ideas presented in this section are derived largely from *Precision Teaching* — a set of techniques developed by Ogden Lindsley at the University of Kansas, and Tom Lovitt, Norris Haring, and their co-workers at the Experimental Education Unit at the University of Washington. We would also acknowledge the contribution of Ted Raybould (University of Birmingham) who was largely responsible for their introduction to the United Kingdom. It is important to stress that there is much more involved in 'precision teaching' than the few ideas presented in these pages, and the interested reader should consult:

Haring, N.G., Lovitt, T.C., Eaton, M.D., and Hansen C.L. (1978). *The Fourth R: Research in the Classroom*, Charles E. Merrill, Columbus, Ohio.

or

Lovitt, T.C. (1977). *In Spite of My Resistance, I've Learned from Children*, Charles E. Merrill, Columbus, Ohio.

As an introductory text the second of these books is more suitable. It has the additional advantage of being witty and enjoyable to read.

Daily measurement can help the class teacher in two ways:

1. Because you are measuring and recording a pupil's performance on a particular objective each day, you are alerted to increases and decreases in the rate of progress — on the very day that it happens. You can therefore avoid prolonged periods of 'non-progress' by adjusting your teaching methods and approaches accordingly.
2. Recording a pupil's daily performance on a chart usually acts as a potent incentive to the pupil to practise and try harder. Pupils should watch the teacher mark up the chart, and some might even be taught to do their own charting. Either way, very few children can resist the challenge of beating yesterday's score.

In practice, it is the second of these benefits which is the most obvious and readily available to the class teacher. As a means of motivating pupils and increasing fluency, charting is almost always effective. Evaluating teaching methods properly by this technique, as the first of these points implies that you can, involves more sophisticated precision teaching procedures.

Daily measurement, remember, is a technique which can help the class teacher to increase a pupil's fluency of performance. It should be used, therefore, only with objectives which have a fluency criterion and during the second phase of teaching — increasing fluency. In other words, we would suggest that daily measurement should not normally be used during the first phase — reducing errors — as this will probably encourage the pupil to attempt a skill at speed which he cannot yet perform accurately. The procedure therefore should not normally be introduced until the pupil reaches the levels of accuracy described in Chapter 5.

The chart

ELSA's Daily Measurement Chart (which may be copied for classroom use) appears on the next page. At the top of the page is space for the pupil's name and the objectives code on which the procedure is to be used. At the foot of the page there is a block of three rows: one marked with a tick, one with a cross, and one for the date. These are to record each day's date and the number of correct and incorrect responses made on each day. You will see that there is space for five weeks recording on the chart with each Saturday and Sunday shaded. The horizontal axis of the chart represents days. Each vertical line which crosses the horizontal axis denotes a different day and (again) the space between each Saturday and Sunday is shaded.

The vertical axis of the chart represents the number of correct and incorrect responses made per minute. It is not calibrated in the usual way — in other words, fifty does not fall midway between nought and one hundred. It is, in fact, semi-logarithmic graph paper, which is another idea taken from precision teaching. Our only reason for recommending its use with ELSA is that it allows a wide range of criteria to be recorded on the same sheet. ELSA's fluency criteria range from twelve responses per minute in A18 and A19 to at least seventy responses per minute in R8. Using 'normal' graph paper, either the vertical axis would need to be calibrated differently according to the fluency criterion of the objective or a range of charts would be required to suit different criteria. Using semi-logarithmic paper this is unnecessary — this one chart can be used with the full range of ELSA objectives.

Using the chart

An explanation of the use of the Daily Measurement Chart will be easier to follow with reference to an example. In Figure 18 there is a completed chart illustrating the progress made by a boy, Jason, on Unit 4 of ELSA Reading.

The first job is to complete the details at the top of the page. You should then draw in the lines to indicate the two aspects of the fluency criterion. In all the objectives in Reading Unit 4 the criteria is forty words per minute with two or less errors. Horizontal lines have therefore been drawn across the page at 2 and 40. The chart is now ready for use.

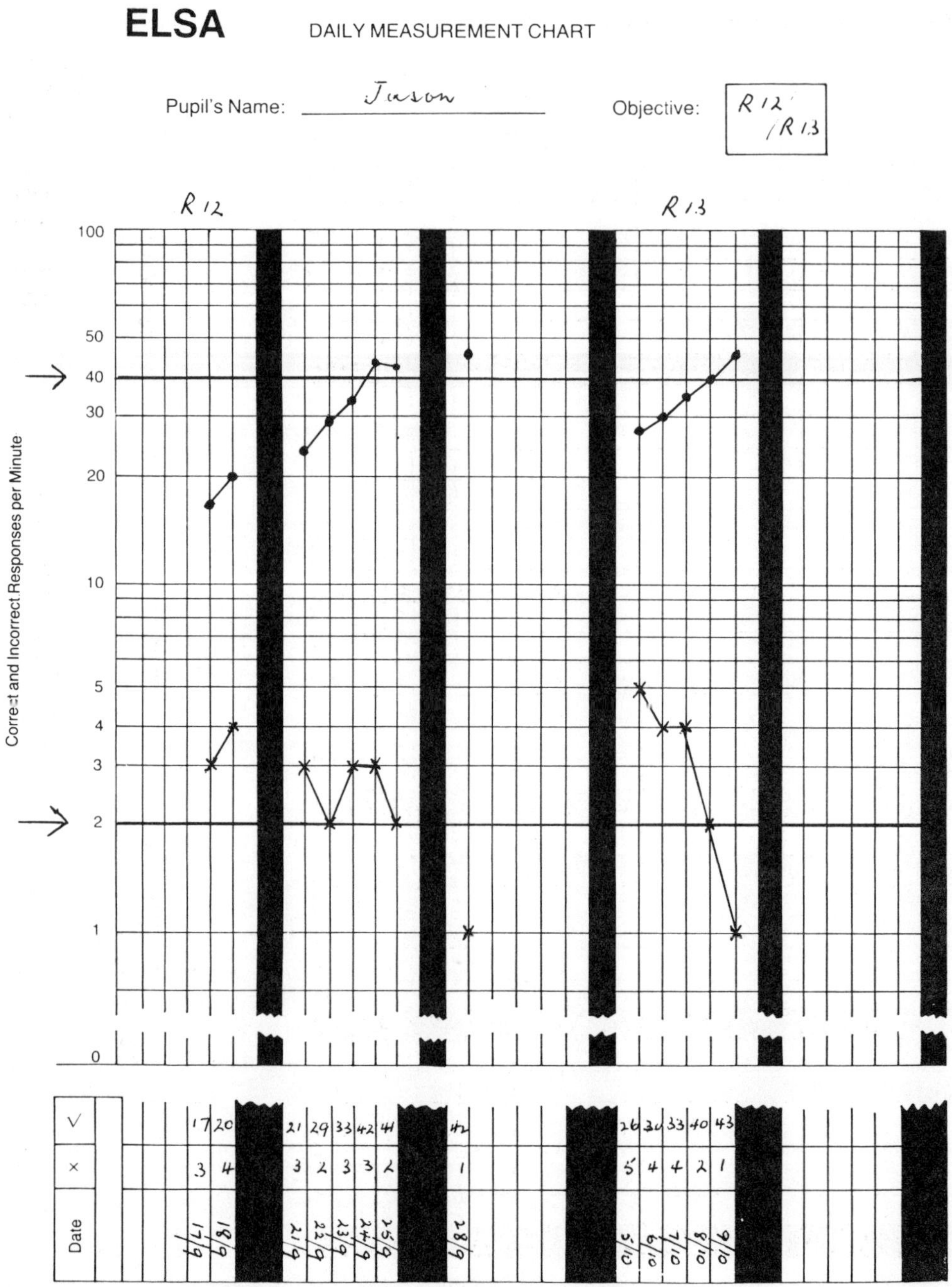

Figure 18

Jason was given Reading Unit 4 as part of his placement test. He made fourteen correct and two incorrect responses on R12, and sixteen correct and one incorrect response on R13. He performed less well on objectives R14 to R17 — making eight or more errors on each. Obviously R12 and R13 should be taught first. On the basis of the above information, however, the class teacher did not know how accurately Jason could perform across the whole range of words in R12 and R13. In the one minute presentations during the placement test Jason had attempted less than twenty words on each.

As a first step, therefore, the class teacher decided to allow Jason to attempt the first forty words on each of these two objectives regardless of the time he took to read them. On both sheets he made less than seven errors. She decided therefore to teach to errors on R12 and R13 until he could read forty correctly with only two errors (i.e. the standard of accuracy contained in the fluency criterion) and then to use daily measurement on each until criteria were reached. Thereafter, she would need to retest Jason on R14 to R17.

Work on R12 was commenced on Thursday 17th September and that date was recorded in the first 'Thursday column' in the bottom row. Jason read seventeen words correctly and made three errors in one minute. This information was recorded in the appropriate rows above the date in Jason's presence whilst the class teacher explained what she was doing and why. She then entered his scores on the graph — a dot for the number of words read correctly and a cross for the number of errors — again explaining what she was doing.

This simple process is repeated each day. The dots are connected with straight lines except across weekends when obviously no data are collected. The crosses are connected in the same way.

ELSA

DAILY MEASUREMENT CHART

Pupil's Name: ____________________

Objective: [ ]

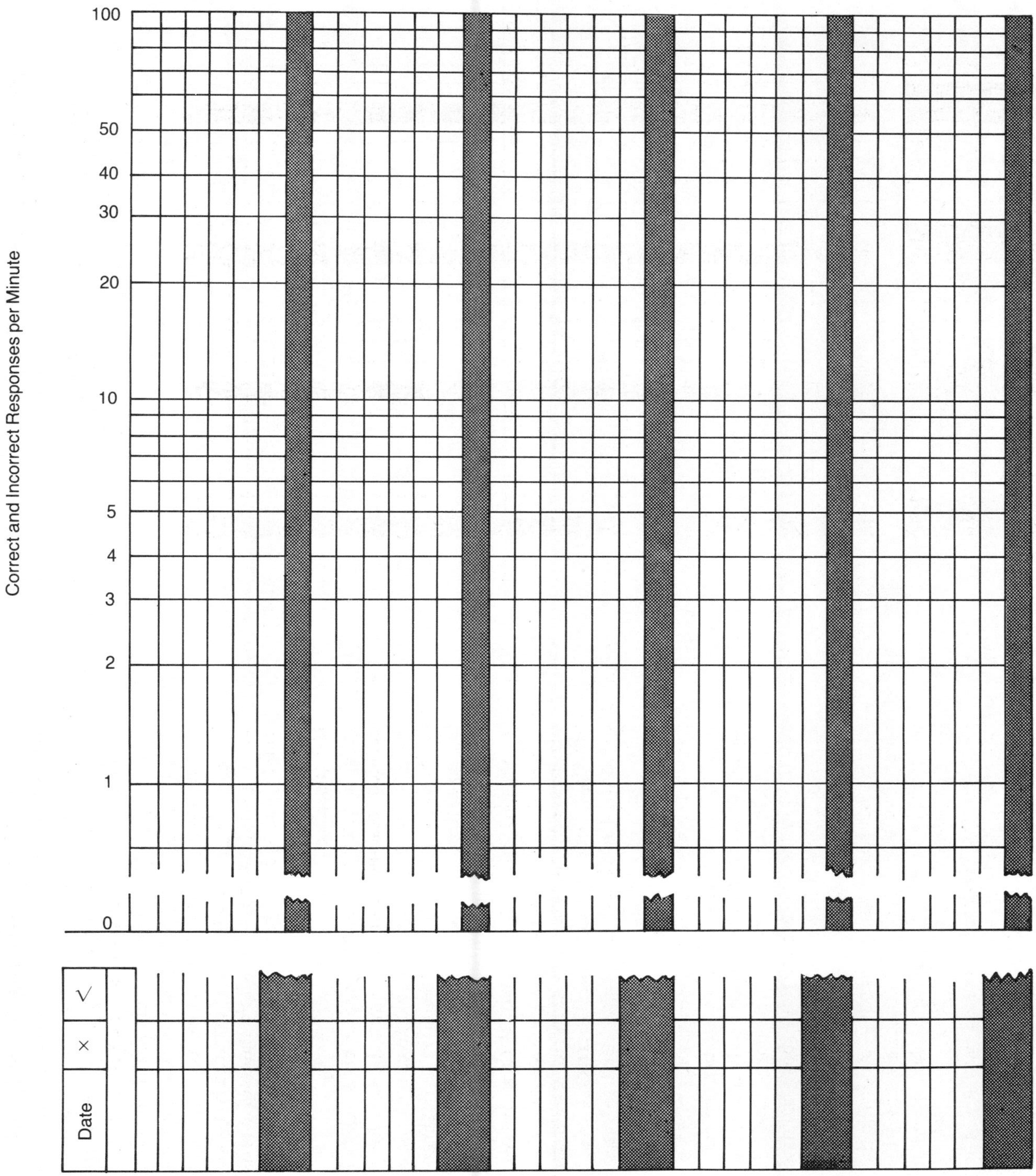

This is all that is involved in daily measurement. Assessing the objective took little more than a minute and recording details of Jason's performance on the chart took a further minute or two — much less than five minutes in total. By definition, however, this has to happen every day and, with reading objectives certainly, it must be done individually.

When the pupil is being introduced to the idea of daily measurement it is important to explain clearly the object of the exercise. This can be done simply using the chart. Pointing to the dots you can say, 'I want you to get the line to go up ... and you can do this by reading *more* words tomorrow than you did today.' Pointing to the target line, say, 'The dots have to reach this line here. If you practise your words and try really hard I'm sure you'll get there very soon.' It is important also to emphasize equally the idea of reducing errors. Say, 'But there's a catch.' Point to the crosses and say, 'I want you to get this line to go *down*, and so tomorrow you must try not to make any mistakes.'

Even very young children usually get the idea quite quickly, although they may not get to the point of being able to chart their own progress. Remember that the main reason for measuring and charting pupils' progress is to motivate the pupil to greater efforts and thus accelerate progress to criteria. It will only have this effect if the pupil has at least some understanding of the purpose of the chart.

Final comment

Daily measurement is a procedure which can help the class teacher to increase a pupil's fluency of performance. It helps in two ways:

1. Because it is a *daily* form of record keeping you are alerted to increases and decreases in the rate of progress on the very day that it occurs.
2. Involving the pupil as much as possible in the charting will usually act as a potent incentive and motivation with most children.

Remember to use daily measurement:

1. Only on objectives which have a fluency criteria and
2. When the pupil reaches the standard of accuracy described in the fluency criterion.

When you are using daily measurement, remember to:

1. Complete the details at the top of the Daily Measurement Chart.
2. Draw in the two horizontal lines to indicate the two aspects of the fluency criterion.
3. Test the pupil on the objective each day and record the date and number of correct *and* incorrect responses made in the three rows beneath the chart.
4. Record the data on the graph using dots for correct responses and crosses for incorrect responses.
5. Join the dots with straight lines — except across weekends — and do likewise with the crosses.
6. Above all, involve and inform the pupil as much as possible in points 1 to 5, and be sure to praise him each day he makes some progress.
7. Repeat the process each day until the recommended fluency criterion has been performed on two successive days.

8

Case Studies

Chapter Goal
To illustrate the use of ELSA by case studies

Case study 1: Simon

Simon started school full-time in September, two months after his fifth birthday, and initially had some difficulty adjusting to classroom life. He had not attended a nursery or playgroup previously. He was prone to tears (particularly when he arrived at school each morning) and could not settle to any one activity for more than a few minutes. Throughout his first two terms in school Simon made very little academic progress.

A few days before the Easter Holiday the class teacher discussed the situation with Simon's mother who reported that she too was worried about his lack of progress, and in particular that Simon continued to be tearful and miserable before setting out for school. In discussion it emerged that Simon's hearing and vision were believed to constitute no problem, and there were no other medical factors which could be adversely affecting his performance in school. They decided to collaborate at the beginning of the Summer Term to teach Simon a sight vocabulary in reading. Simon's mother expressed a willingness to help in whatever way she could and they agreed to meet after the holiday to plan a course of action.

On 28th April the class teacher administered the ELSA placement test for Reading Unit 1. Objectives R1 to R3 are items for which no assessment materials are provided. She began by writing down five words which Simon said he could read — 'mommy', 'daddy', 'Simon', 'aeroplane', and 'Mick'. She found, in fact, that he could only read the first three of these. This information was recorded on the ELSA Records which appear in Figure 19.

Next, the class teacher found a tin which she labelled 'Simon', and put inside it three flash cards of the words which Simon could read. She explained that when he learnt a new word she would write it on a card and put it in the tin, and that he could take this tin home to show his parents each evening.

The next day the class teacher saw Simon's mother and gave her two sheets of notes explaining how she might help at home. She had produced these handouts (which appear in Figures 20 and 21) during the Easter Holiday specially for Simon, but felt certain that they would subsequently be useful with other children and their parents. On the same day she began teaching the words 'this is' (on one flash card) so that he could now read three sentences — 'this is mommy', 'this is daddy', and 'this is Simon'. Moreover, he could attempt to copy these sentences under pictures of his family which he had painted and these were later displayed on the classroom wall. A few days later the flash card 'this is' was added to Simon's tin.

A week later, on 6th May, when the class teacher was certain that the five words in Simon's

Simon

	Materials	Instructions	Pupil Performance	Recommended Criteria	Placement Test	Record (Date): Working on	Mastered	Checked
R1	The following ten words each presented on an individual flash card: *mommy daddy Simon this is Rachel our house Mick dog*	'Read these words aloud.'	**Reads aloud ten words**	10/10	*28th April* √ X	*29/4*	*15/5*	*29/5*
R2	The ten flash cards from R1, presented three times	'Use these words to make a sentence ... What does it say:' Dismantle the sentence and repeat	**Builds and reads aloud three sentences,** each containing at least three words	3/3	√ X	*18/5*	*19/5*	*29/5*
R3	The ten words from R1, plus the following ten words, each presented on an individual flashcard: ______ ______ ______	'Read these words aloud.'	**Reads aloud twenty words**	20/20	√ X	*22/5*		

Notes/Comments

'Mummy', 'daddy', and 'Simon' known on 28.4.81. Use flash cards and tin. Parents?

Figure 19

ELSA READING Unit 1

Suggestions for Parents

If your child brings home a tin of flash cards you can help him to learn them with the activities described below.

1. Place the cards (face upwards) on the floor or table. Then say: *'Point to the card which says ________'.* If he points to the correct card, praise him and put the card back in the tin. If he points to the wrong card, show him the correct one but do *not* allow it to be put back in the tin. Come back to that card later. Continue until all the cards are back in the tin.

OR 2. Hold the cards in a pile and present them one by one saying: *'What does this one say?'* If he gets it right, praise him and put the card back in the tin. If he gets it wrong, tell him the correct answer and put that card at the bottom of the pile for another attempt later. Continue until all the cards are in the tin.

OR 3. Once there are ten or more words in the tin you can lay the cards down face upwards and practise building sentences. These should be very simple sentences of three, four, or five words. Always ask your child to read aloud the sentence when it has been constructed.

Figure 20

ELSA

Practical Hints for Parents

There are a number of general points to bear in mind when working at home with your child.

1. *Work for only five or ten minutes*— even if your child wants more. Say: 'If you're good, you can do some more tomorrow.' Remember that lots of short sessions are better than a few long sessions.
2. *Never bully your child to work at home.* Try to present the activities as games — to be enjoyed.
3. *Praise your child for effort and correct answers.* Show him that you are pleased and that you think he is doing well.
4. *Never lose your temper or become impatient* if your child gets something wrong. If that's the way you feel, try again some other time when you're in a better mood.
5. *Always end on a winning note.* Finish each session with a question or task which you know your child can answer or perform satisfactorily.
6. *If you have any problems, call at school and ask.*

Figure 21

tin had been mastered, the words 'Rachel', 'our', and 'house', were introduced. Again, these words were Simon's choice and they were used to label paintings done in class. 'Mick' (Simon's dog) and 'dog' were added a few days later, and on 14th and 15th May Simon read all ten words aloud without error.

The work carried out with Simon can be related to the first two of the three phases of teaching described in Chapter 5. Much of the teacher's effort was concerned with the first phase, working with him until he could read aloud the words without error. The parents' role, on the other hand, was one of providing extra practice in order to increase fluency (i.e. phase two). Clearly this is an example of the idea of the phases of teaching being used flexibly. Simon was involved in phase two on some of his words whilst at the same time working on reducing errors with others.

This simple case study did not involve either of the advanced techniques in Chapter 7; nor did it involve the class teacher in extensive individual teaching. Nevertheless, it illustrates a number of the advantages inherent in ELSA:

1. Simon's difficulties were spotted early, and an intervention was planned and implemented promptly by the class teacher.
2. The class teacher, using the ELSA placement test, began by finding out exactly what Simon could do in reading.
3. She worked to clearly defined teaching objectives, concentrating initially on reducing his errors.
4. Precise and detailed records of the intervention were kept.
5. The pupil's parents, having expressed a willingness to help, were given detailed and practical advice on how they could support the school's efforts by helping to increase fluency of reading.

Case study 2: Marcia

Marcia, who is the youngest of four children in her family, attends a large inner city primary school. In September, when she was six and a half years old, she went into the top class of the Infant Department. She was having some difficulties in most academic aspects of the curriculum, but was at least *as* competent as a group of six or seven other children in her class, all of whom were receiving withdrawal help in reading and number work.

Within two or three weeks of the commencement of the Autumn Term the class teacher became concerned about a different aspect of Marcia's behaviour in school — her apparent inability to follow instructions in the classroom. Typically, she would carry out only half an instruction, or be unable to find or replace equipment after the class teacher had described its whereabouts. Moreover, Marcia was an accomplished gymnast and athlete for her age, but frequently she could not carry out a described exercise or activity in PE until another pupil had provided a demonstration.

Marcia's class teacher sent a note home asking her mother to call at school to discuss the situation. In particular, she wanted to confirm that Marcia's hearing was satisfactory and that there were no other medical or physical factors which might be affecting her work. Mother reported that Marcia was extremely healthy and that she had not noticed any difficulties in hearing. Nevertheless, permission for a hearing test to be carried out at school was given and the class teacher assured Marcia's mother that she would get in touch as soon as there was anything to report.

A hearing test was arranged and carried out two or three weeks later. The test detected no abnormality of hearing and Marcia's mother was informed of the result.

Marcia

	Materials	Instructions	Pupil Performance	Recommended Criteria	Placement Test	Record (Date): Working on	Mastered	Checked
L18	Pictures illustrating five spatial concepts (i.e. on, in, under, next to, in front of)	For each picture: 'Where is the ___?'	**Uses five spatial concepts**	5/5	28.10.81 √ 2 X 3	2.11.81	18.11.81	27.11.81
L19	Pictures illustrating five spatial concepts (i.e. behind, between, near, over, inside)	For each picture: 'Where is the ___?'	**Uses five more spatial concepts**	5/5	29.10.81 √ 1 X 4	16.11.81	27.11.81	11.11.81
L20	Pictures illustrating the following five spatial concepts: below top beside through above.	For each picture: 'Where is the ___?'	**Uses five other spatial concepts**	5/5	√ X	30.11.81	7.12.81	11.12.81

Notes/Comments

L.18 Correct under and next to
L.19 correct inside

Figure 22

The class teacher next decided to assess Marcia's understanding and use of language using ELSA. Over a period of a week she administered Units 3, 4, 5, and 6 of ELSA Language as a placement test. The objectives in Unit 3 (Same and Different) and Unit 4 (Colours and Shapes) were all performed to the recommended criteria. Marcia made four correct responses out of five in L16 (Adverbs), but had considerable difficulties in Unit 6 (Spatial Concepts). These data seemed to tie in with the class teacher's observations of Marcia's difficulties in PE in particular.

It was the policy of the school which Marcia attended to spend a lot of time on oral language work, and there was a well-developed Language Resource Area in the school. The placement test results indicated, however, that Marcia needed intensive individual attention on particular aspects of language. The class teacher decided therefore to 'teach to the errors' on L18 and L19,

ELSA LANGUAGE Unit 6

Suggestions for Parents

To play this game you will need a flat surface and five or six different small objects (e.g. cardboard box, toy car, spoon, pencil, cup, and a piece of paper). It doesn't matter what the objects are, providing your child knows their names.

This is a game to help your child learn some important words and phrases which describe where objects are in relation to each other. These will include 'under', 'in front of', 'behind', 'next to', and several more. I will tell you which words and phrases to practise when I see you.

1. Say: *'I want you to do exactly what I say. Are you ready?'*
   Then, speaking clearly and slowly, give an instruction like:

   'Put the spoon NEXT to the car.'
   'Put the car BEHIND the box.'
   'Put the pencil UNDER the paper.'

   If your child follows your instruction praise him. If he doesn't, show him and give him another try.

2. This time, *you* put the spoon next to the car, and ask: *'Where's the spoon?'* The answer you want is 'Next to the car'. Or, *you* put the car behind the box, and ask: *'Where's the car?'* The answer you want is 'Behind the box'. Again, if he gets it right praise him. If he doesn't, tell him the answer and give him another try.

Figure 23

and to invite Marcia's mother to help. The results of the Unit 6 placement test (and Marcia's subsequent progress) appear in Figure 22.

On 2nd November the class teacher met Marcia and her mother together at the end of afternoon school. She gave her the handout which appears in Figure 23 and the list of general hints for parents in Figure 21. She explained briefly how the arrangement was to work. Marcia agreed to work at home with her mother for five minutes each evening, and the three agreed to meet each Monday afternoon to review progress. The particular spatial concepts to be practised at home were to be supplied by the class teacher each Monday.

Work on Unit 6 began on 2nd November and was completed on 11th December. There were six Monday afternoon meetings, each lasting only ten or fifteen minutes. During this period the class teacher never spent more than five minutes per day working individually with Marcia, but after only six weeks Marcia knew fifteen important spatial concepts which helped her considerably in following the teacher's instructions.

The class teacher took particular care also to seek opportunities for Marcia to apply the concepts she had learnt in a variety of situations, as recommended in Chapter 5. In PE lessons particularly she made careful plans to put Marcia in situations where she alone was required to follow simple instructions involving the use of these spatial concepts.

As in the first case study this example uses no sophisticated teaching methods, but again the steps taken by the class teacher were appropriate and realistic. The basic checks were carried out, in particular to rule out the possibility of a problem of hearing. A detailed assessment of Marcia's difficulties in language was undertaken, specific areas of need were identified, and precise teaching objectives were set. Finally, detailed records of the intervention were kept, and the efforts of school and home were properly coordinated.

Once again you should also note the flexible application of the three phases of teaching described in Chapter 5. Phase one was represented by the teacher's intensive individual instructions to teach Marcia to understand and use the spatial concepts with a minimum of errors. The mother's contribution was to do with the second and third phases — increasing fluency and applying the skill to a variety of materials.

Case study 3: Jason

Jason was seven years four months when he started junior school. He was a cheerful lad who was popular with both teachers and pupils. Standardized tests, administered a few weeks before he left infant school, indicated that he was reading as well as an average pupil of about six. His number work was at a comparable level. Despite his difficulties, Jason clearly enjoyed school and always tried hard. His parents had responded only once to several invitations to visit the infant school to discuss his progress. He was obviously extremely healthy, and his vision and hearing had been checked twice during his final year in infant school.

After a term in junior school Jason's class teacher decided that a special effort should be made to improve his spelling. Jason was making slow but measurable progress in other curriculum areas, but his spelling was becoming a major problem.

ELSA	SPELLING
UNIT **2**	SOUNDS, BLENDS, AND COMBINATIONS

Child's Name JASON ROBERTS

ENTRY SKILLS: Reading Unit 3; attention must also be paid to the relationship with individual objectives in Reading Unit 4

TEACHING OBJECTIVES:

S4	Writes letter sounds from dictation	/
S5	Writes ten consonant–vowel–consonant words from dictation	2 =
S6	Writes ten more consonant–vowel–consonant words from dictation	2 =
S7	Writes ten words with common final consonant blends from dictation	4
S8	Writes ten more words with common final consonant blends from dictation	
S9	Writes ten words with common initial consonant blends from dictation	
S10	Writes ten more words with common initial consonant blends from dictation	
S11	Writes ten words with final 'e' from dictation	
S12	Writes ten more words with final 'e' from dictation	

MATERIALS REQUIRED:
Sheets of words from pages 187 to 190

Figure 24

The class teacher was confident that Jason had no sensory or medical difficulties which needed investigation. She consulted the topsheets for the three ELSA Spelling units and decided to administer Unit 2 (Sounds, Blends, and Combinations) as a placement test. She noted that the recommended entry skills for this unit included an ability to *read* the words in ELSA Reading Unit 3 (Letter Sounds and Simple Blends) and Unit 4 (Blends and Combinations). She was quite sure that Jason could read these words, but quickly checked by asking him to read the words in the objective R17 — the longest (and probably the most difficult) words in the unit.

Jason's records and details of placement test performance appear in Figures 24, 25 and 26. The class teacher was able to carry out the placement test during one session since she decided not to ask him to attempt all nine items in the unit. This was because of his apparent distress at not being able to spell the words in the objective S7.

Following the guidelines recommended in Chapter 4 she then decided upon a teaching order for the four objectives with which she was concerned and recorded this on the unit topsheet. Objective S4 was to be taught first since Jason only made a few mistakes on this task. Consequently the teacher's approach was to teach to errors, giving him short individual sessions on the three letters that were causing difficulty; this proved to be successful.

When it came to objectives S5 and S6, however, Jason's poor results on the placement test indicated that he was still very much at the stage of needing to reduce errors. She decided, therefore, to produce a more detailed teaching programme using the idea of slicing. The programme she produced is presented in Figure 27 and consists of seven steps in which the sixty words from R11 are presented a groups of twelve on the basis of their medial vowels. Included in the programme are two revision items (i.e. S5.03 and S5.06). To assist her with the actual teaching she printed the groups of words on a series of cards.

The class teacher next needed to decide on her methods of teaching, given that she could not rely on Jason's parents to help and she could afford to spend very little time herself working individually with Jason. She decided to teach Jason a little routine which would enable him to teach himself, and involve her merely in checking that his work had been done properly. He was to spend ten minutes each day on spelling practice. He needed his current card of twelve words, a sheet of lined paper, and a pencil. For each word on his list he was told first to copy the word, then to turn over his sheet of paper and the card, and try to write the word from memory. He could finally check his attempt against the card, tick it or do his correction, and go to the next word. Jason quickly learnt this simple sequence: copy – cover – write – check. When he had worked through

Jason

	Materials	Instructions	Pupil Performance	Recommended Criteria	Placement Test	Record (Date): Working on	Record (Date): Mastered	Record (Date): Checked
S4	Paper and pencil	'Write down these sounds …b, as in ball.' Present letter sounds in random order.	Writes letter sounds from dictation	26/26	19th Jan; √ 23, X 3	19th Jan.	27th Jan.	31st Jan.
S5	The following ten words from R11: ______ ______ ______ Paper and pencil	'Write down these words: ______'	Writes ten consonant – vowel – consonant words from dictation	9/10	19th Jan; √ 3, X 7	27th Jan	7th March	
S6	The following ten words from R11: ______ ______ ______ Paper and pencil	'Write down these words ______'	Writes ten more consonant – vowel – consonant words from dictation	9/10	19th Jan; √ 2, X 8	27th Jan	7th March	

Notes/Comments: 19th Jan. – Jason needs work on h, p, and q sounds
27th Jan. – Using task analysis programme

Figure 25

the list Jason knew how many of the twelve words he had spelt correctly first time, and the class teacher merely checked each day that the task had been performed correctly.

Every two or three days, when it seemed that Jason had learnt his list, the class teacher tested him by reading out the twelve words on the card. If Jason spelt at least eleven of these correctly on two consecutive days he was given the next card in the sequence. After working through three or four cards in this way, the class teacher involved Jason in deciding when he was 'ready' for the test, a simple strategy which seemed to have the effect of encouraging him to work even harder.

Using this procedure Jason eventually achieved the criteria for S5 and S6. It took almost a term, during which time Jason spent about ten minutes nearly every day working on his own. For most of these days the class teacher was involved for only two or three minutes when checking his work or testing an objective.

Once again this example illustrates how ELSA can be incorporated into the teacher's daily classroom routines. She established what Jason could and could not do in spelling. On the basis of the placement test data she decided which objectives needed further attention and the order in which they should be taught. She developed appropriate teaching materials and a system for teaching which could be managed in her classroom. Finally, she kept detailed records of Jason's progress throughout the programme.

Case study 4: Sharon

Early on in her junior school Sharon was identified as a pupil who was experiencing considerable difficulty in Maths. Under the guidance of the school's educational psychologist she was provided with extra help in a withdrawal group taught by a part-time remedial teacher. Initially the staff had some difficulty in deciding where to place Sharon within ELSA Arithmetic since her attainments seemed to be so scattered. They found, for example, that despite her poor performance on certain objectives to do with number concepts (e.g. A5 and A8) she was able to carry out some simple addition sums (i.e. A9).

After some discussion it was decided to take Sharon back to the early units and ensure that she could carry out all the objectives to the criteria levels recommended. This tactic seemed to pay off since Sharon proceeded through the various units at a good pace: by the time she reached Unit 6 she had grown in confidence.

On the timed placement test for Unit 6 Sharon's results were as follows:

	√	X
A18	8	2
A19	6	1

	Materials	Instructions	Pupil Performance	Recommended Criteria	Placement Test	Record (Date)		
						Working on	Mastered	Checked
S7	The following ten words from R12: ______ ______ ______ Paper and pencil	'Write down these words: ______'	**Writes ten words with common final consonant blends from dictation**	9/10	19th Jan √ 1 X 9			
S8	The following ten words from R12: ______ ______ ______ Paper and pencil	'Write down these words: ______'	**Writes ten more words with common final consonant blends from dictation**	9/10	√ X			
S9	The following ten words from R13: ______ ______ ______ Paper and pencil	'Write down these words: ______'	**Writes ten words with common initial blends from dictation**	9/10	√ X			

Notes/Comments: 19 Jan. – Concluded placement test on item S7 since Jason is out of his depth.

Figure 26

To get a clearer picture of Sharon's level of accuracy on these items the class teacher then allowed her to attempt all the sums on each of the two sheets without any time constraint. She was encouraged to find that under these less pressurized circumstances Sharon completed almost all the examples with only an occasional mistake.

The class teacher then discussed the placement test results with the educational psychologist and the remedial teacher and they agreed that opportunities would be provided for Sharon to practise the appropriate levels of sum in her book every day in order to increase fluency. She would also be allowed to carry out similar exercises using a computerized toy. To monitor this the remedial teacher was to see Sharon each day to carry out regular assessments using the daily measurement procedures described in Chapter 7. They felt that this might help to maintain her level of enthusiasm during this period of what was largely routine drill and practice.

The plan was in line with the recommendations made earlier about the use of daily measurement. The procedure can be used, you will recall, on teaching objectives which have a fluency criterion once the pupil can perform the skill to the level of accuracy described in the recommended criterion.

As can be seen on the Daily Measurement Chart presented in Figure 28, Sharon's fluency increased at a satisfactory rate. Look carefully at the data. On the objective A18 her initial reaction to being asked to speed up her work seemed to be to do more sums but with a much higher rate of errors. However, once the need for speed *and* accuracy was stressed her progress towards the required level of performance was rapid. A similar effect can be seen to some extent on A19.

Sharon, like many children who have been introduced to the idea of daily measurement, found it to be an enjoyable way of increasing her fluency. The daily testing was carried out in a friendly, relaxed way, and no particular pressure was applied other than to draw attention to the previous day's performance and encourage her to improve on it.

This example shows how ELSA was used to provide appropriate instruction, matched carefully to the particular needs of one pupil for a period of just over two weeks on the basis of a few minutes of a teacher's time per day. In most normal classrooms ELSA is a set of procedures to be used *some* of the time with *some* of the

ELSA Pupil: JASON ROBERTS.

	Ten randomly selected words from R11	'Write down these words......'	Writes ten consonant-vowel-consonant words from dictation.	9/10

Code	STEPS TO OBJECTIVE S 5/6	Records		
		Working on	Mast-ered	Checked
S 5.01	Writes from dictation twelve short 'a' words (11/12)	27th Jan	31st Jan	
S 5.02	Writes from dictation twelve short 'e' words. (11/12)	31st Jan	4th Feb	
S. 5.03	Writes from dictation twelve words. Chosen randomly from S.5.01 and S.5.02. (11/12)	4th Feb	7th Feb	11th Feb
S. 5.04	Writes from dictation twelve short 'i' words. (11/12)	7th Feb	11th Feb	
S. 5.05	Writes from dictation twelve short 'o' words (11/12)	11th Feb	18th Feb	
S 5.06	Writes from dictation twelve words chosen randomly from S 5.03, S 5.04, and S. 5.05. (11/12)	18th Feb	28th Feb	1st March
S 5.07	Writes from dictation twelve short 'u' words. (11/12)	28th Feb	7th March	

Figure 27

pupils. Its strength is seen as facilitating the efficient use of the class teacher's limited resources of time. In this example it also provided the basis for a cooperative initiative geared to providing extra support to a pupil with special needs using daily measurement to increase fluency.

Case study 5: group reading

The emphasis throughout our description of how to use ELSA had tended to be on working with individuals. In this case study, a brief account is given of how part of ELSA Reading was used with a group of eight to ten year olds in a primary school. The eleven pupils, drawn from different classes in their school because of their poor reading attainments, were maintained on the programme by one teacher. Having been assessed on the objectives in Reading Units 3 (Sounds and Simple Blends) and 4 (Blends and Combinations), each pupil was seen individually each day for four minutes.

Before the project began the sheets of words for objectives R10 to R16 were task-analysed using slicing so that new words were taught in groups of six. The following simple daily procedure was used:

1. *Recording error words*. Each pupil had his own word book. Only one copy of the ELSA assessment (and additional word) sheets were required, which the teacher kept and used with all the pupils. The pupil was asked to read aloud, without timing, the sheet related to his current objective. Any words which the pupil could not read were recorded, with the date, in his word book, and practice provided on these.
2. *The one-minute timed trial*. The pupil was then asked to read aloud as many words as he

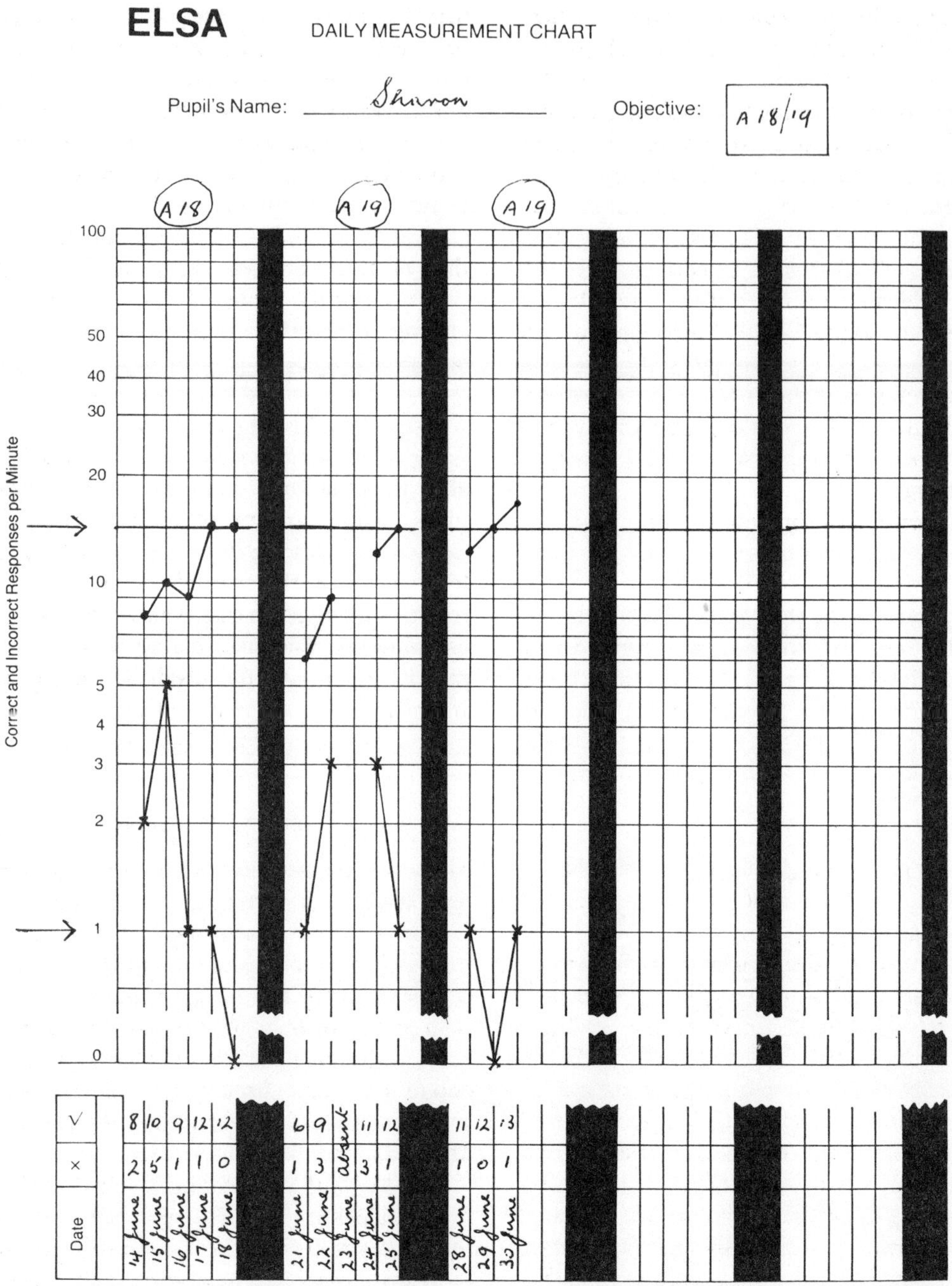

Figure 28

could in one minute. Accuracy and speed were emphasized equally. The number of correct and incorrect responses were counted and recorded. (Note that procedures 1 and 2 were sometimes combined, so that errors could be recorded during the timed trial.)

3. *Charting pupil progress*. The day's performance was then graphed, with the pupil at least watching and (if possible) helping. Completing the chart usually only took a minute and, without exception, acted as an enjoyable and potent incentive for the pupil to learn new words.

Before the project began the class teachers of the pupils involved were told exactly what was going to happen. For their part they were asked simply to find two to five minutes each day to practise one or more of that day's error words from the pupil's word book. They were not asked to prepare special materials, keep records, or even set aside a regular time for this work.

At the outset, too, the parents of the eleven children were invited to school for an evening meeting, and were asked to spend between five and ten minutes each evening practising that day's words. General advice on how to go about this was provided; in particular, they were told never to bully their child into practising but always to make it enjoyable by playing memory games of various types and to try to end the session on a positive and successful note.

The project lasted for seven months. Although the progress of the eleven pupils involved was measured and charted each day, a more comprehensive evaluation of the procedures was undertaken. In particular, standardized tests were used to measure increases in pupils' reading ages and questionnaires were used to tap the attitudes and reactions of the parents and class teachers of the children.

The reading ages of the eleven pupils increased by an average of ten and a half months during the seven-month period of the project, according to the Burt (Rearranged) Word Reading Test. Pre- and post-testing using the Neale Analysis of Reading Ability indicated average increases in excess of ten and a half months (during the same seven months) on accuracy, comprehension, *and* rate of reading. Of course, we cannot be one hundred per cent. sure that these impressive results were not brought about by some other factors quite unrelated to the programme. However, the reading ages of these same pupils were more than two years below their chronological age at the beginning of the project. For whatever reason their *rate* of progress increased dramatically.

Arguably, what is as important as these test results was the reactions of pupils, their parents, and class teachers. The feedback from questionnaires was unreservedly positive. All the children were said to have enjoyed taking part, most were more likely to read books voluntarily at home, and general improvements in attitude and confidence were reported for most of the children.

The results of this small study indicated the potential for increasing pupils' attainments when teaching programmes were carefully matched to existing attainments and when the efforts of pupils, parents, and class teachers were coordinated and directed.

Case study 6: language development project

This example concerns the use of ELSA within the context of curriculum development. It describes how ELSA Language was adapted and developed as part of a school's overall language development programme.

The school in question caters for children with moderate learning difficulties. After some of the teachers in the primary department had used ELSA Language with individual pupils they decided to incorporate it as part of the school curriculum in order to establish a greater sense of continuity and consistency in their teaching of this crucial area. They accepted, of course, that this material only represented one aspect of their school's language policy but nevertheless felt that the objectives were of particular relevance to many of their pupils.

In order to adapt ELSA Language to the precise needs of their pupils the staff involved met on a regular basis under the direction of the Deputy Head. The school's educational psychologist and speech therapist were also invited to these meetings.

Over a period of some weeks the teachers reviewed the objectives presented in ELSA Language, adapting them where they felt it to be necessary. In so doing they added extra items to some of the units and, indeed, incorporated two new units. Having agreed the overall structures of the programme they went on to redesign much of the assessment material using their own illustrations and, where appropriate, concrete items. Finally, a set of these assessment materials was made available in each of the primary classrooms, including booklets for recording pupil progress along similar lines to the ELSA record sheets.

As the staff began to implement their version of ELSA Language with the children they became aware of the need for extensive teaching materials geared to the objectives, particularly in order to achieve a reasonable degree of generalization. The next stage of the project, therefore, was a series of practical workshops at which the members of staff analysed the extensive range of commercially produced teaching materials available within the school in an attempt to relate them to their programme. To facilitate the use of the programmes a language resource centre was established in an area adjacent to the classrooms. Here the teaching materials were boxed and marked with the code of objectives to which they related. Where obvious gaps were apparent the teachers designed and produced a range of relevant visual materials using magazine pictures and photographs taken around the school and its neighbourhood. By the time all this work was completed the staff were understandably proud of their resource centre and very committed to the language scheme they had developed.

Using ELSA as the basis for a scheme which a group of teachers can follow is particularly valuable in situations, such as special schools or units, where groups of children with similar needs are working together. It is important, however, as in the example described here, that teachers involved in this type of initiative should examine the objectives carefully with a view to matching them to the needs of their pupils. It also makes sense to work collectively in developing a range of relevant teaching materials.

Case study 7: in-service training

Much of the material presented in this book has been used on in-service courses for teachers and is presented in a format which will lend itself to use as a basis for a series of workshops. One such course followed the model recommended, with each participant carrying out practical classroom assignments with one child. Towards the end of the course discussion focused on teaching to objectives and, in particular, the idea of three phases of teaching.

The teachers on the course felt that they had been able to use the first two phases effectively, finding short periods during each day to work on reducing errors, as necessary, and developing supplementary materials and activities for increasing fluency. A number also involved parents in providing additional practice at home. The main problem they found was to do with the third phase — applying skills. They argued that leaving this crucial aspect to chance or simply waiting for opportunities to arise was unsatisfactory. Consequently it was agreed that an extra session of the course should be arranged to look in detail at possible phase three activities.

The discussions centred on the teaching objectives involved in the various ELSA programmes used by each participant. Working in small groups they considered ways in which these skills could be applied in a variety of relevant situations once a satisfactory level of fluency had been achieved. To facilitate the exercise they found it useful to write new objectives. The following examples illustrate some of the issues raised:

1. *Handwriting*. In this case the teachers looked at ways of applying the handwriting skills taught in H4, H5, and H6. The teacher concerned was aware that despite the improvements in her pupil's writing within the context of the timed assessment sessions his written work in other lessons was still poor. After a lot of discussion it was agreed that the pupil should be told that each day one fifty-letter sample of his ordinary written work would be judged for legibility against an example of his best handwriting. These samples might be taken during any class activity which involved handwriting. Daily scores would be kept indicating the number of correct letters out of fifty. The objective was:

Materials	Instructions	Pupil performance	Recommended criteria
Selected samples of the child's handwriting with at least fifty letters	None	**Writes Legibly**	48/50

2. *Language*. A child who had mastered L10 would be able to discriminate between the colours of similar pairs of objectives. The course participants felt that the next stage in applying this skill would be to work on pairs of dissimilar objects. They therefore recommended that the pupil in question should work towards the achievement of the following objective:

Materials	Instructions	Pupil Performance	Recommended criteria
Five pairs of dissimilar objects, i.e. ball — book pen — pencil hat — scarf car — boat milk — juice Two pairs the same colour	For each pair: 'are these the same colour or different?'	**States whether colours are same or different**	5/5

3. *Reading*. Reading Unit 4 consists of six teaching objectives, each of which concentrates on one particular type of phonic blend or combination. In discussing the application of these skills the teachers felt that it was important to monitor their use during normal reading activities. They suggested that a list of the various phonic conventions should be kept handy when hearing the child read in order to note examples of their use. In addition, they decided that it was necessary to provide systematic practice on materials where the child was required to discriminate between examples of the different types of words taught. Consequently they produced an extra assessment sheet involving a selection of the words from each of the six teaching objectives, presented in random order. Their new objective was:

Materials	Instructions	Pupil Performance	Recommended criteria
Sixty different words from R12 to R17 (ten from each, randomly arranged). Present for one minute	'Read these words quickly, trying not to make mistakes.'	**Reads aloud words from Unit 4**	40 per min Max. 2 errors

As can be seen from these examples, the discussions led to an analysis of important issues with regard to the third phase of teaching ELSA objectives. We felt that it was a particularly successful in-service experience and would recommend it to others developing a course along the lines recommended in this book.

ELSA Assessment Material

A4

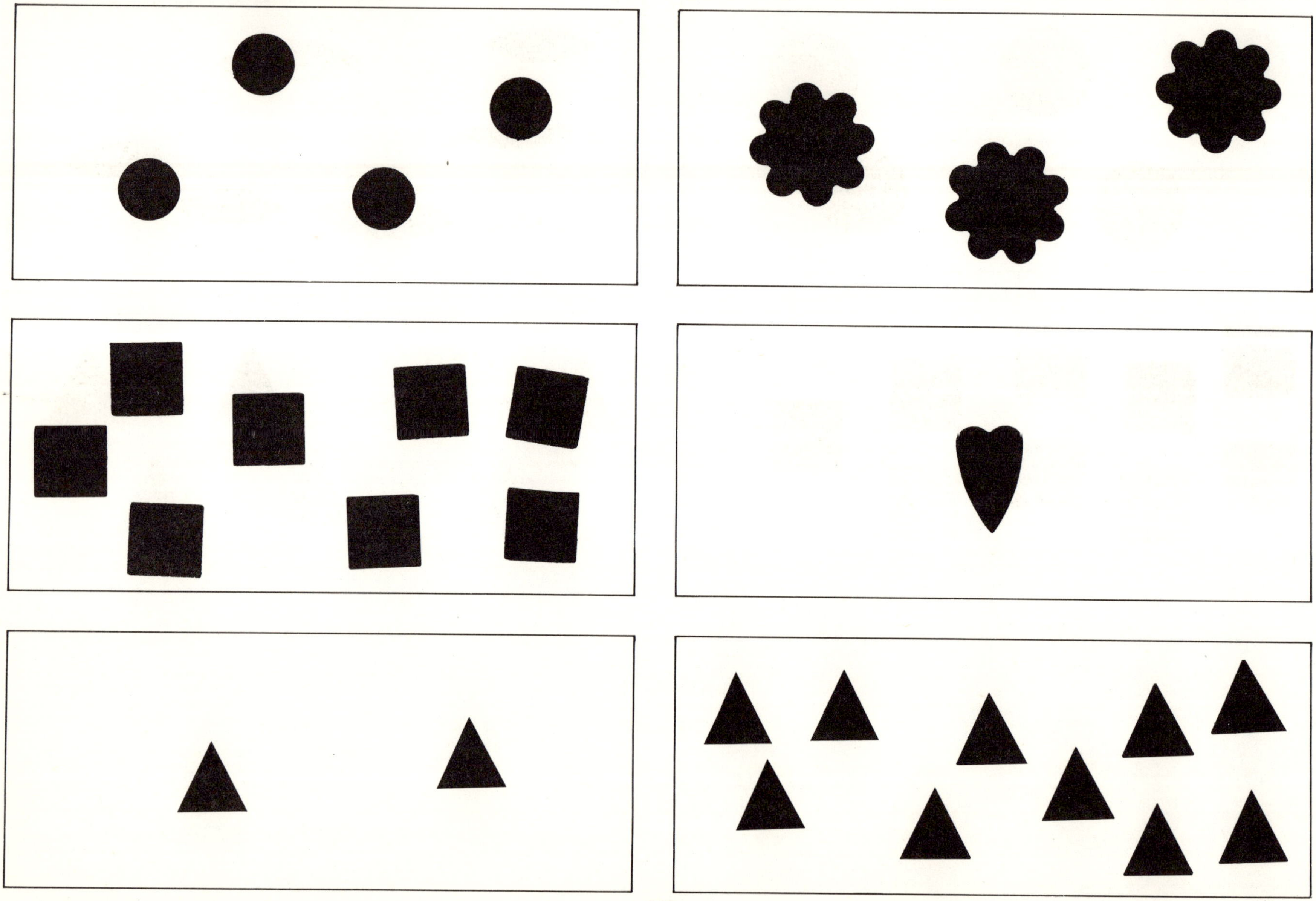

A4

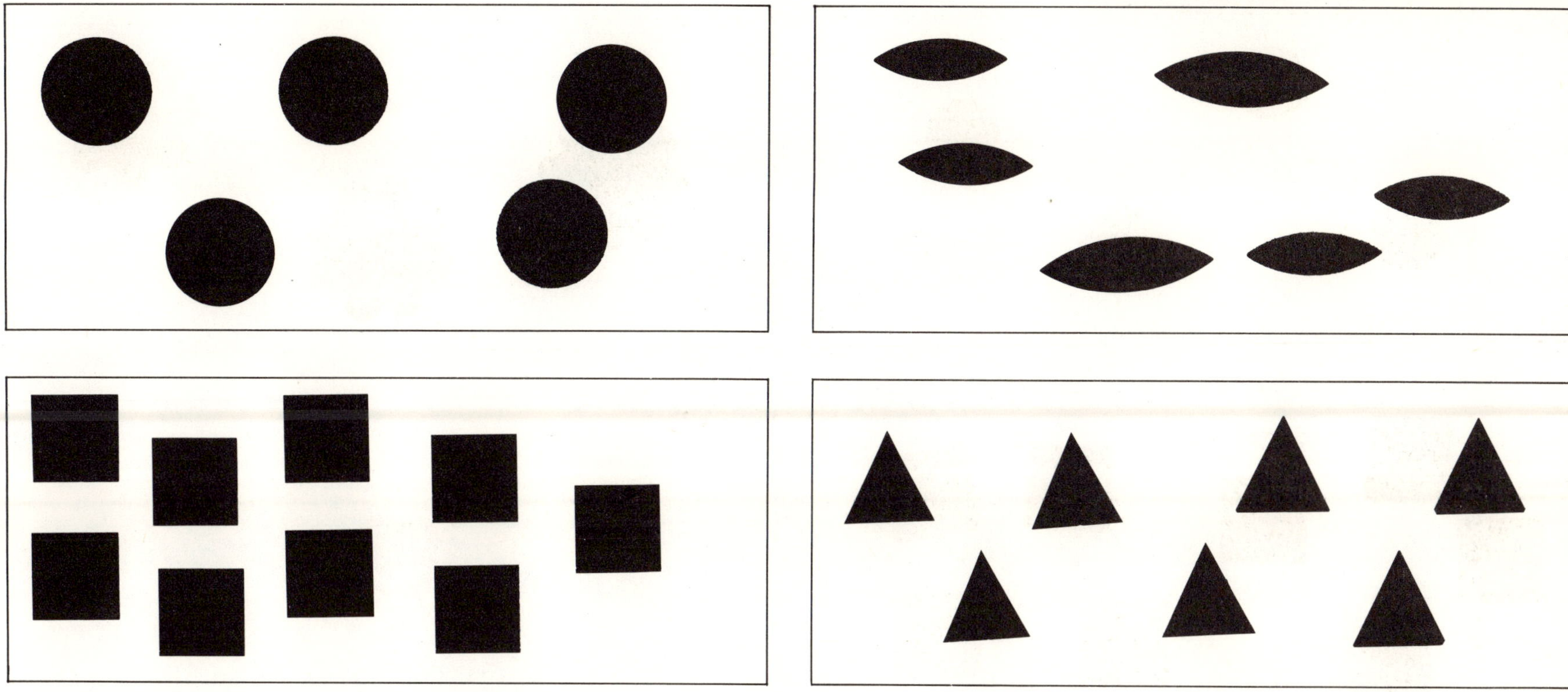

A6

7	10	5	2	1	0	(6)
6	4	8	3	9	1	(12)
10	2	9	3	4	8	(18)
7	5	8	0	7	10	(24)
5	2	1	0	6	4	(30)

A9

5 + 4 =	6 + 3 =	2 + 7 =	(3)
0 + 9 =	7 + 3 =	4 + 6 =	(6)
3 + 3 =	1 + 4 =	2 + 1 =	(9)
2 + 8 =	8 + 1 =	10 + 0 =	(12)
2 + 5 =	6 + 4 =	0 + 0 =	(15)
1 + 8 =	8 + 2 =	1 + 9 =	(18)
5 + 2 =	1 + 7 =	2 + 2 =	(21)
7 + 3 =	1 + 4 =	3 + 0 =	(24)
2 + 6 =	9 + 1 =	5 + 4 =	(27)
0 + 5 =	3 + 6 =	2 + 0 =	(30)

A10

5 - 0 =	7 - 1 =	8 - 7 =	(3)
10 - 5 =	6 - 0 =	8 - 3 =	(6)
6 - 2 =	2 - 1 =	3 - 1 =	(9)
9 - 3 =	5 - 4 =	7 - 5 =	(12)
8 - 5 =	10 - 0 =	4 - 3 =	(15)
9 - 4 =	9 - 8 =	6 - 5 =	(18)
9 - 9 =	6 - 3 =	8 - 0 =	(21)
4 - 4 =	3 - 2 =	8 - 2 =	(24)
10 - 9 =	10 - 7 =	4 - 2 =	(27)
10 - 10 =	2 - 0 =	5 - 3 =	(30)

A11

$\square + 5 = 10$	$5 + \square = 7$	$\square + 6 = 8$	(3)
$\square + 1 = 9$	$4 + \square = 5$	$\square + 3 = 6$	(6)
$7 + \square = 10$	$3 + \square = 9$	$\square + 5 = 8$	(9)
$\square + 2 = 6$	$\square + 1 = 8$	$1 + \square = 4$	(12)
$\square + 2 = 10$	$\square + 4 = 5$	$1 + \square = 7$	(15)
$\square + 2 = 9$	$\square + 2 = 5$	$8 + \square = 8$	(18)
$\square + 9 = 10$	$\square + 2 = 4$	$0 + \square = 6$	(21)
$4 + \square = 9$	$\square + 4 = 7$	$2 + \square = 3$	(24)
$4 + \square = 10$	$\square + 9 = 9$	$1 + \square = 6$	(27)
$3 + \square = 8$	$\square + 0 = 2$	$4 + \square = 7$	(30)

A15

11	15	20	19	13	16	(6)
12	18	14	17	16	18	(12)
12	11	15	17	13	20	(18)
19	14	15	18	17	20	(24)
11	13	12	19	14	16	(30)

A18

19 + 0	4 + 13	8 + 5	9 + 4	10 + 7	12 + 2	5 + 15	(7)
9 + 9	9 + 5	7 + 4	17 + 2	8 + 8	6 + 5	10 + 10	(14)
2 + 15	6 + 6	0 + 20	10 + 5	11 + 3	10 + 1	10 + 6	(21)
13 + 1	9 + 2	14 + 5	7 + 5	8 + 3	3 + 15	3 + 12	(28)
7 + 12	19 + 0	16 + 1	11 + 1				(32)

A19

15	13	11	19	14	16	18	
- 3	- 6	- 0	-12	- 9	- 7	- 1	(7)
17	11	18	16	13	19	15	
- 1	- 4	-18	-14	-11	-15	- 5	(14)
12	18	16	13	14	18	12	
- 9	- 8	- 8	-10	- 2	-10	- 2	(21)
11	20	17	11	20	17	14	
-10	-19	- 6	- 7	-13	-15	-14	(28)
18	14	17	18				
- 7	- 3	- 0	-15				(32)

A20

8 + 1 =	5 + 2 =	8 - 4 =	(3)
5 - 1 =	10 - 6 =	6 + 3 =	(6)
3 + 4 =	3 - 3 =	8 - 1 =	(9)
4 + 2 =	10 - 8 =	5 - 5 =	(12)
6 + 0 =	9 - 2 =	0 + 4 =	(15)
1 + 6 =	1 - 1 =	4 + 0 =	(18)
3 - 0 =	5 + 5 =	2 + 7 =	(21)
7 + 2 =	6 - 4 =	7 - 6 =	(24)
8 - 6 =	10 - 2 =	3 + 1 =	(27)
9 + 0 =	6 - 1 =	9 - 5 =	(30)

A22

11 − 4	10 + 2	1 + 12	13 − 6	13 + 3	17 − 2	14 − 8	(7)
14 + 0	2 + 17	11 + 9	20 − 4	16 + 10	15 − 3	2 + 16	(14)
12 − 9	6 + 11	8 + 8	14 − 9	4 + 10	18 − 7	20 − 15	(21)
6 + 13	18 − 5	5 + 14	9 + 8	15 − 6	19 − 7	16 + 4	(28)
14 + 13	12 + 8	17 − 8	16 − 6				(32)

A23

3 0 14 + 2	12 5 + 1	3 11 + 4	6 10 + 2	7 2 + 8	(5)
4 6 1 + 7	4 7 + 6	6 0 + 4	4 3 + 12	0 14 + 5	(10)
11 3 4 + 0	9 6 + 3	5 5 + 10	9 8 + 0	9 2 + 9	(15)
10 6 1 + 2	16 1 + 2	10 1 + 7	8 4 3 + 5	9 2 + 8	(20)

H1

a b c d e f g h i

j k l m n o p q r

s t u v w x y z

H2

0 1 2 3 4 5 6

7 8 9 0 1 2 3

4 5 6 7 8 9

H3

A B C D E F G H I

J K L M N O P Q R

S T U V W X Y Z

H4

The children are going

home today with their

Mummy and Daddy.

H4

They had been on

a holiday with their

uncle at the seaside.

H5

Write these words neatly on another piece of paper. Thank you.

Take care as you write all the letters. Do not forget the spaces.

You will need to be able to write neatly. All it needs is practice.

L4

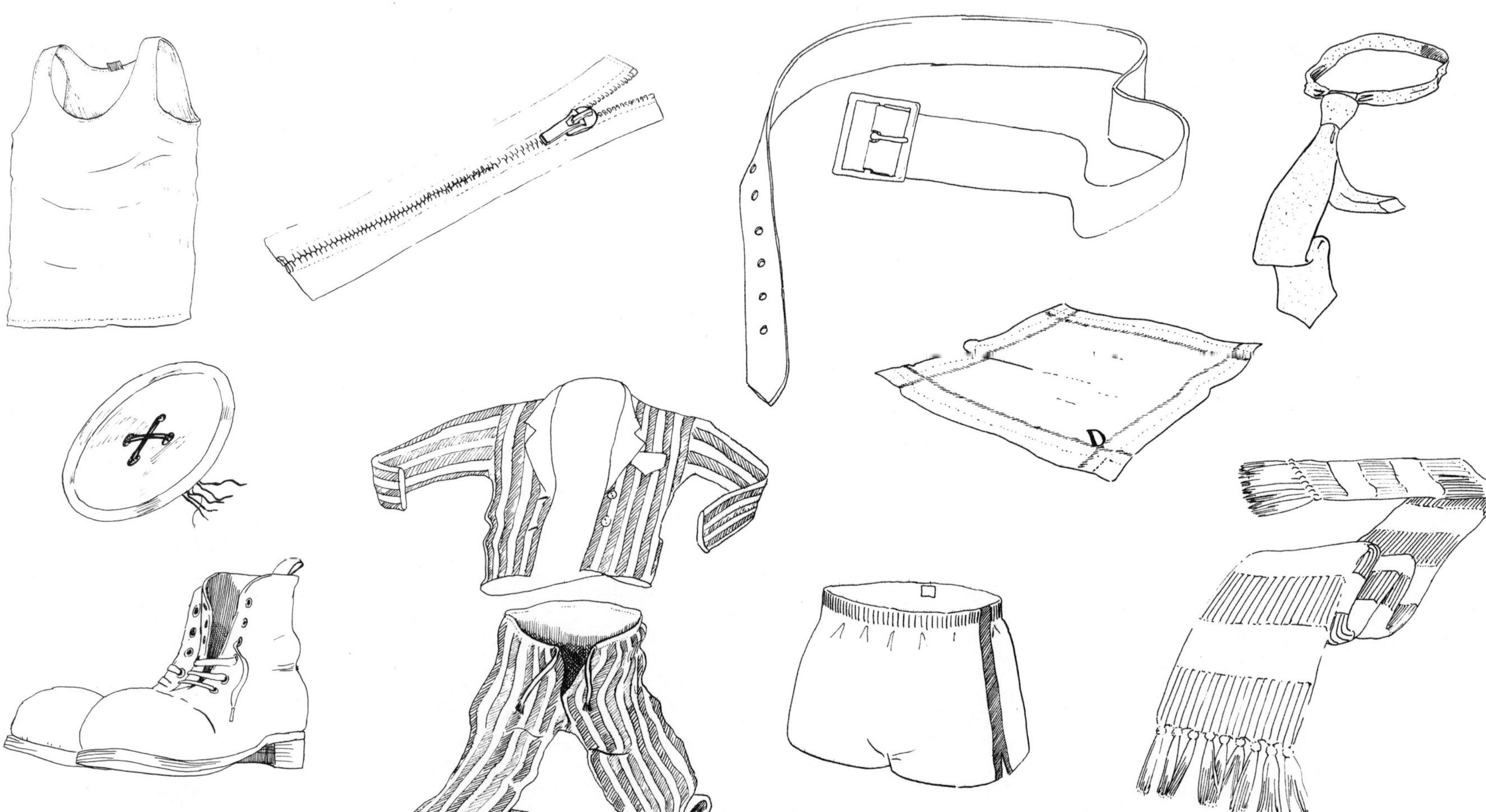

L6

L7

L7

L7

L8

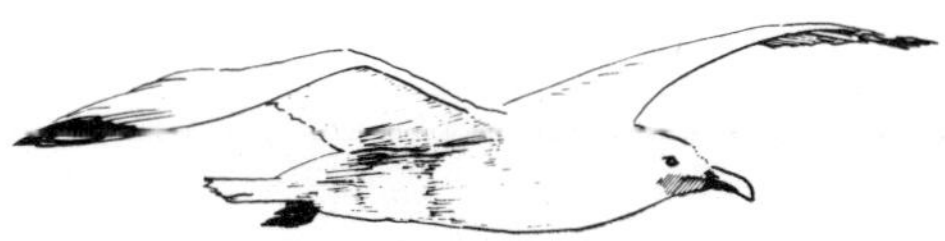

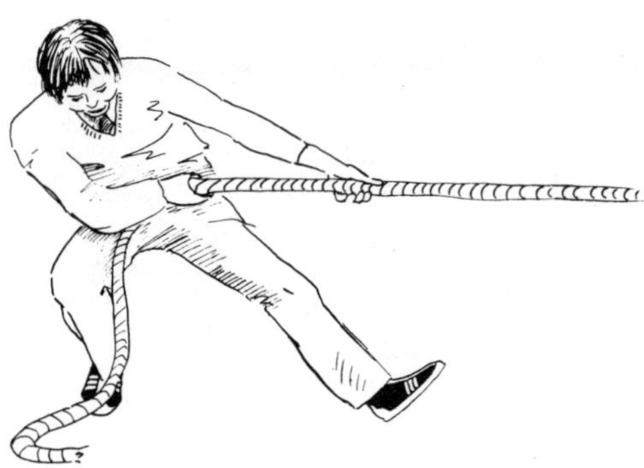

L8

L8

L18

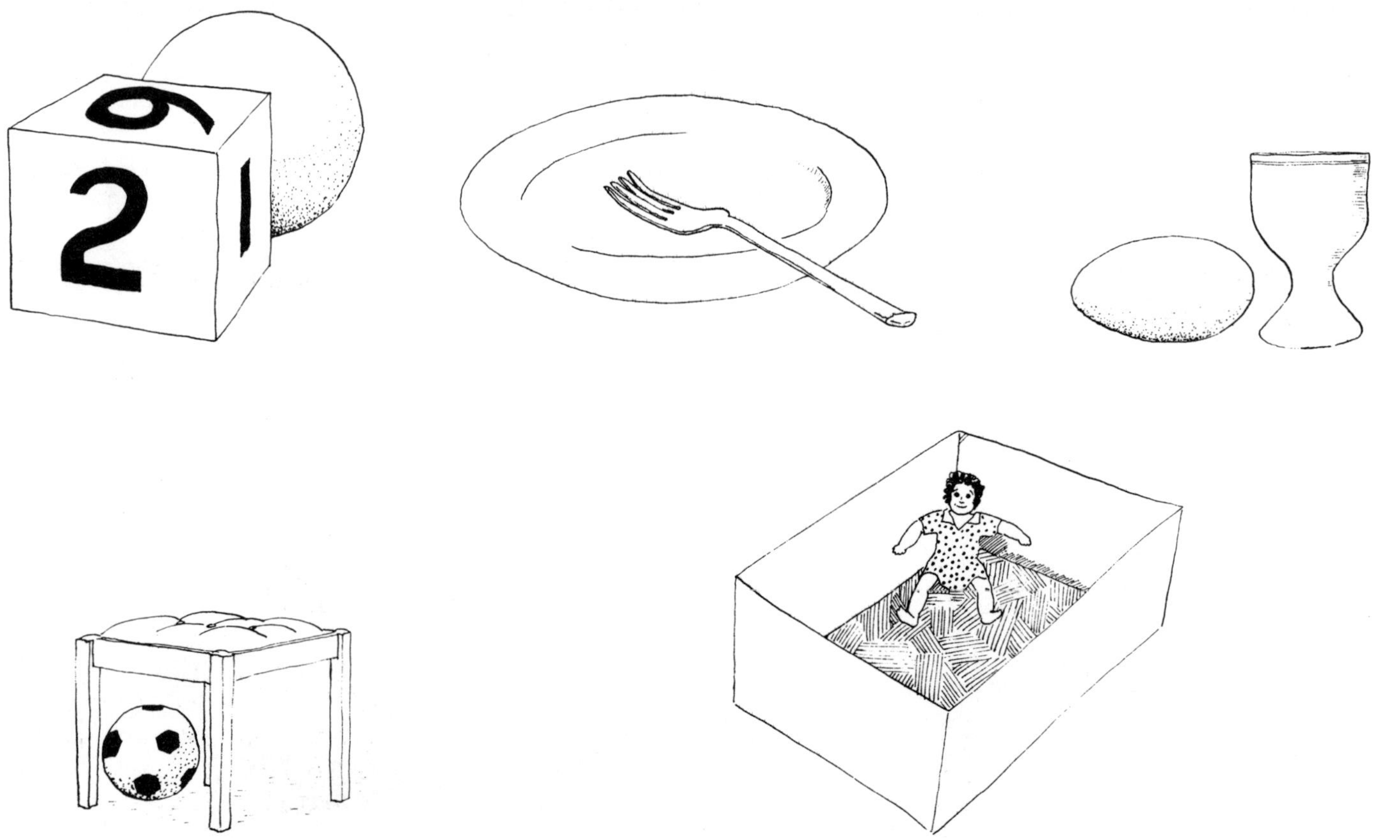

L19

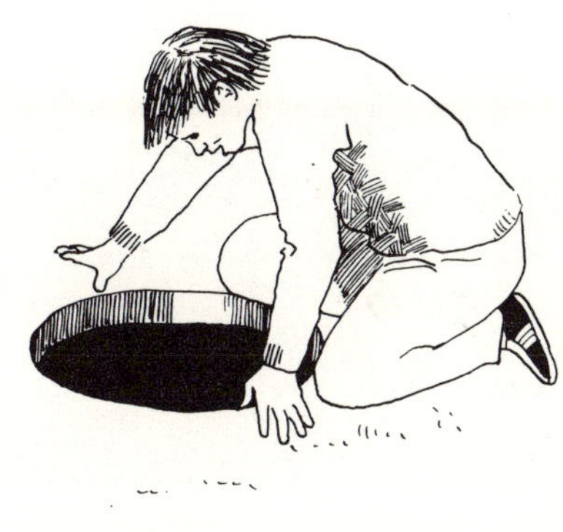

L27

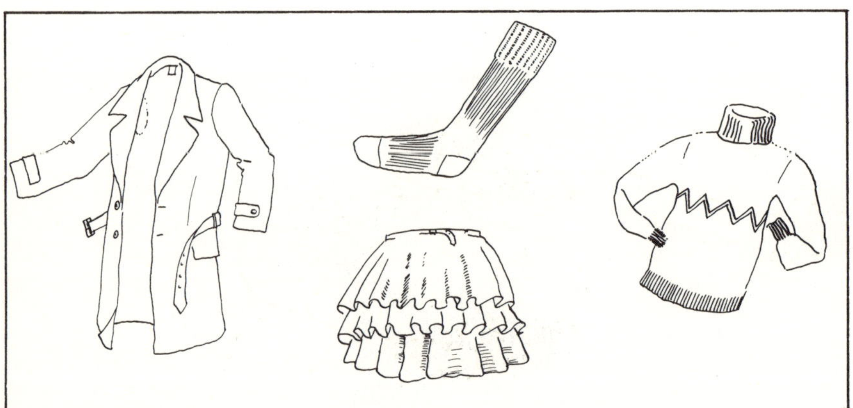

L27

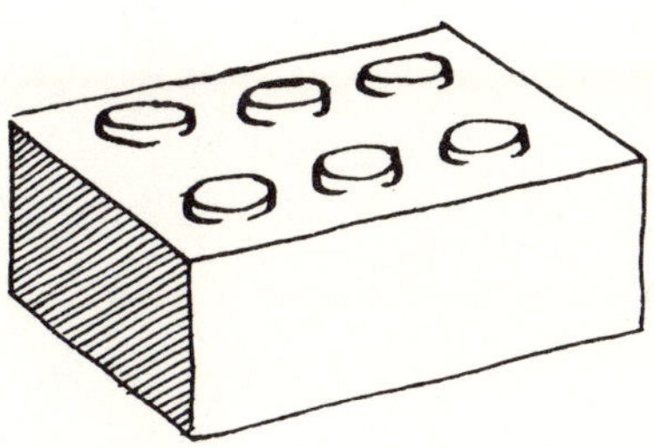

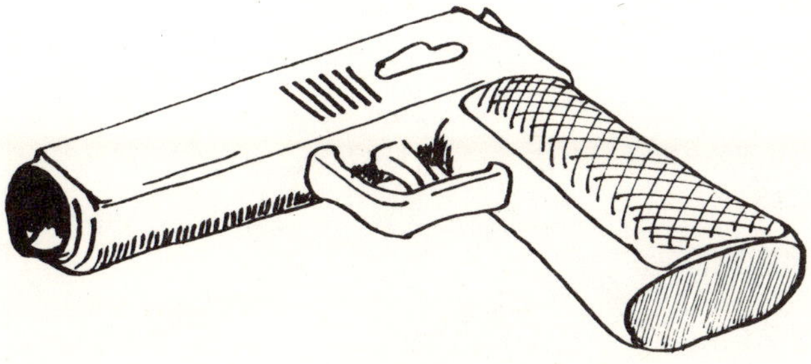

L28

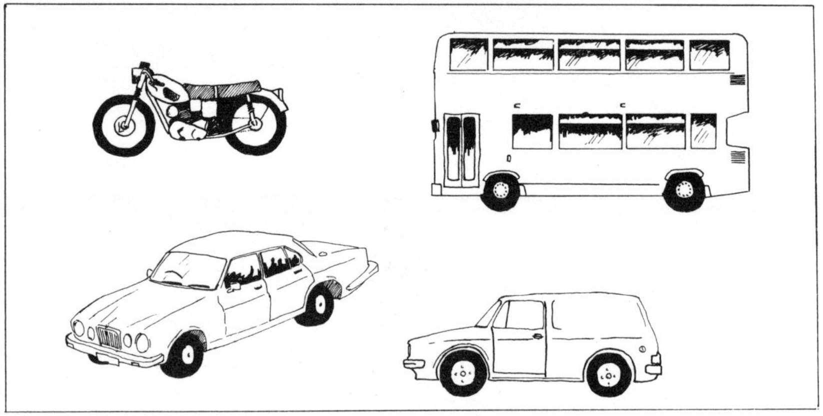

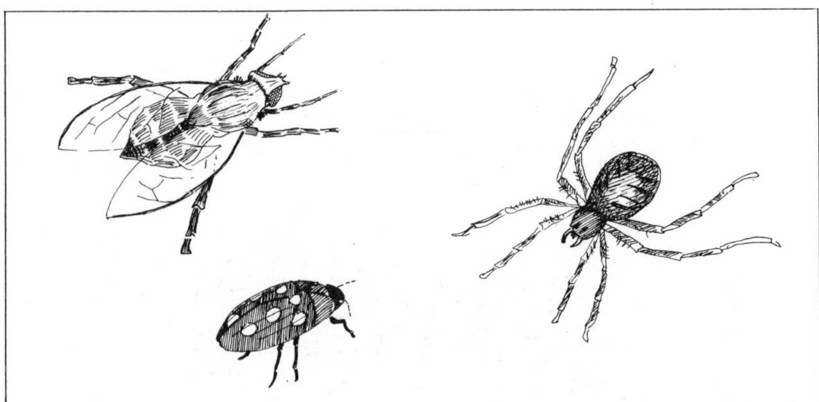

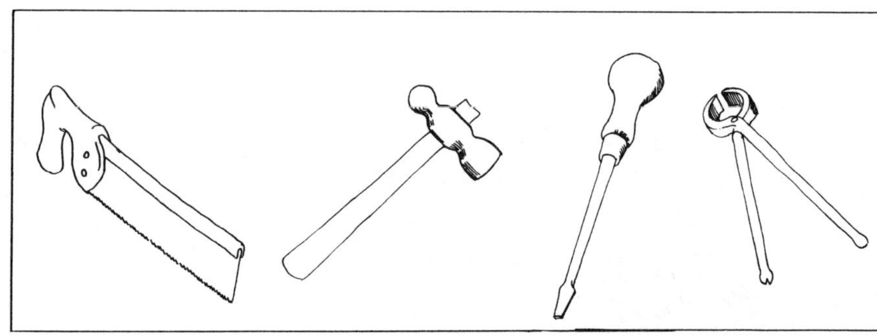

L28

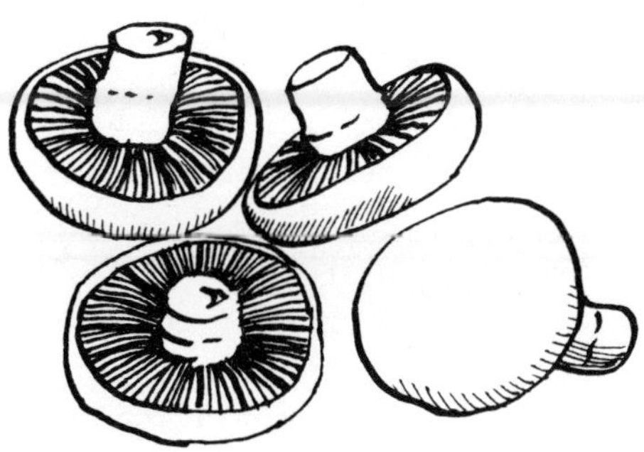

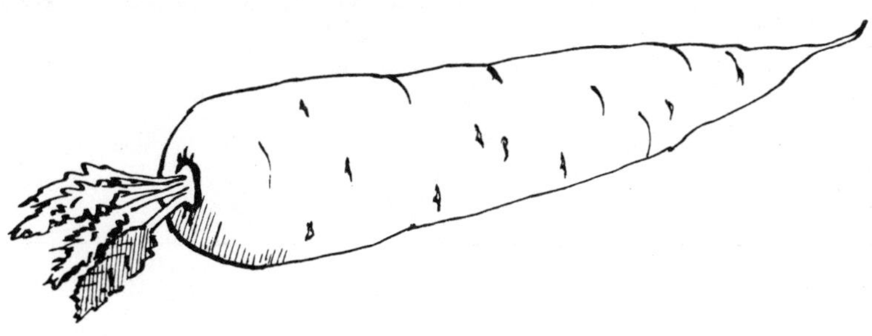

L36

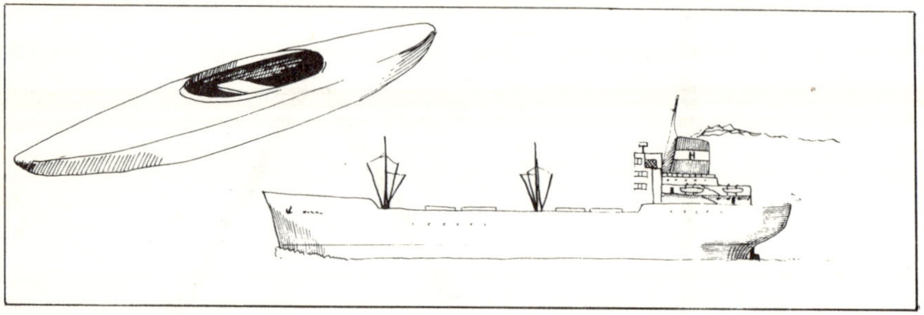

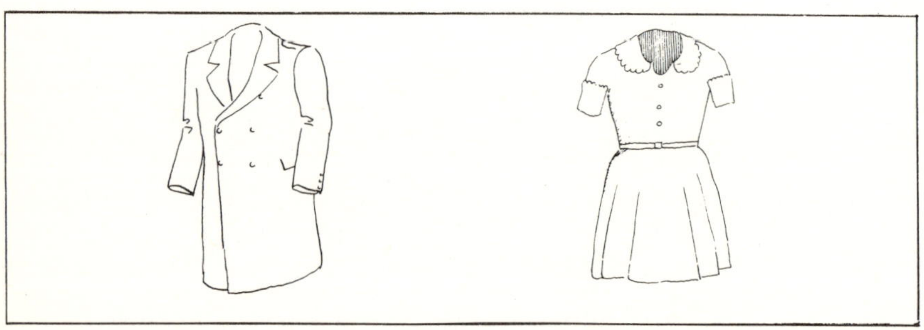

M9/10

R7/8/9

Notes on reading assessment (i.e. R7, R8, and R9)

It will be necessary to prepare assessment materials related to the reading scheme, or schemes, used in your school. Examples are presented here for Book 3A in the Ladybird series (used with the permission of the publisher). The same approach has been used to prepare assessment materials for a variety of commercial schemes.

R7 is a sheet listing all the new words a child will need in order to read the book, assuming that he has read earlier books in the series.

R8 is a passage taken from the book, which the child will be expected to read at a suitable rate (in this case, seventy words per minute with a maximum of two errors). Fluency rates for particular books can be based upon observation of children who are considered to be competent. For most books a rate of something like eighty to a hundred words per minute, with no more than two or three errors, is recommended. Lower rates should, of course, be accepted from pupils who have articulation difficulties.

R9 is a list of comprehension questions, including acceptable responses. Different types of questions should be included, e.g. recall, sequence, and interpretation. It is important to read all the comprehension questions to the child *before* he reads the passage since we want to examine his level of understanding, not his memory.

When preparing assessment materials for longer books, it is wise to choose a number of passages and sets of questions from different parts of the story.

R7

Word List L3A

play	up	at	down	on	(5)
boat	see	get	me	cake	(10)
please	station	train	with	rabbits	(15)
one	that	man	help	Mummy	(20)
Daddy	car	good	Police	an	(25)
apple	give	flowers	red	boys	(30)
was	bus	girls	school	tea	(35)
bed	on	down	red	at	(40)
boys	up	was	play	bus	(45)
cake	girls	me	school	get	(50)
tea	see	bed	boat	please	(55)
Mummy	flowers	give	train	apple	(60)

R8

Fluency Passage L3A

Jane and Peter like to help Mummy. (7)

They go to the shops for Mummy. (14)

I like to shop, says Jane, it is fun. (25)

Come on, Peter says, we have to go to the fish shop. (35)

Yes, says Jane, it helps Mummy. (41)

Peter and Jane like to help Daddy. (48)

They help Daddy with the car. (54)

Jane is in the car. (59)

Daddy and Peter have some water. (65)

Peter likes to play with water. (71)

I like it, he says, it is fun. (79)

R9

COMPREHENSION SHEET L3A.

1. What was the story about?
   (helping Mummy and Daddy)

2. How did Peter and Jane help Mummy?
   (they went to the shops)

3. Which shop did they go to?
   (fish shop)

4. What did they help Daddy with?
   (car)

5. Do you think Mummy and Daddy were pleased? Why?
   (yes, because Jane and Peter helped)

R10

k	a	j	d	o	b	(6)
e	y	x	p	d	g	(12)
b	z	p	f	n	l	(18)
k	j	z	w	s	i	(24)
q	q	h	g	r	i	(30)
o	l	c	f	r	v	(36)
s	e	w	d	u	x	(42)
n	u	e	t	a	o	(48)
t	b	m	p	v	h	(54)
u	c	i	y	m	a	(60)

R11

cat	red	zip	dog	sun	bed	(6)
run	hot	sit	bat	pen	van	(12)
fix	hop	jug	pal	jet	cup	(18)
got	tin	fat	ten	bit	rob	(24)
sum	men	can	but	big	cot	(30)
bin	let	lot	cut	jam	not	(36)
nut	dad	mix	yes	tug	pet	(42)
job	bag	dig	tap	leg	gun	(48)
top	mop	bad	lip	fun	get	(54)
wet	man	rod	pig	gum	did	(60)

R12

hand	held	sank	kept	gulp	gasp	pond	(7)
tilt	mask	fact	self	nest	end	help	(14)
sulk	raft	lamp	punk	and	hunt	golf	(21)
left	last	desk	mend	felt	tank	lift	(28)
jump	mint	wink	send	tent	soft	milk	(35)
act	gift	went	mist	lump	must	pink	(42)
sand	damp	bent	film	lost	bump	pant	(49)
best	belt	camp	dust	sink	sent	limp	(56)
ink	melt	hint	fast				(60)

R13

crab brim spit slot stop grab trap (7)

drop from skin flag crop slit stab (14)

grip trip drum fry skip flap plod (21)

slip stem grit try drip frog skid (28)

fly plug pram bled clip crib spot (35)

slap stun smug slim scan twig sly (42)

blot glum clap prim plan snap flop (49)

sky drag trot grin swim smog step (56)

slug spin brag cry (60)

R14

late here hole rule take mine home (7)

pure bake bike Pete page like cure (14)

joke hope hide rude gate time note (21)

eve save tide tame cute nose mile (28)

rope fade bone side use make kite (35)

mule made ripe cone wave gaze hose (42)

fume tape size mate yoke fire pole (49)

tile mute hate rose wire bite same (56)

fine line rode dive (60)

R15

paid	shed	this	seat	ring	wash	hurt	(7)
nail	hang	neat	sing	laid	that	turn	(14)
shop	bath	heat	fish	sail	wing	near	(21)
path	bang	burn	pain	shin	curb	tail	(28)
then	year	song	rain	the	curl	dish	(35)
fail	them	read	king	ship	meal	gain	(42)
rush	purr	lung	with	weak	pail	surf	(49)
shut	long	aim	ear	rung	bead	raid	(56)
fur	shot	fear	meat				(60)

R16

hard	feet	book	sour	chop	for	arm	(7)
weep	food	loud	such	born	star	seem	(14)
soon	out	chug	feed	tool	farm	beef	(21)
dark	chat	bout	torn	feel	pork	cart	(28)
much	fool	part	noon	pout	seed	chap	(35)
port	cool	chin	barn	our	been	fort	(42)
park	rich	cook	moon	heel	took	need	(49)
farm	lark	see	chip	pool	sort	keep	(56)
room	harm	corn	peep				(60)

S13/14/15

The following list of fifty words is based upon the *Alphabetical Spelling List* (ASL) but compiled to: (1) contain words which appear frequently in childrens' reading books and (2) exclude words which contain common letter combinations taught in other units.

all	also	any	are	as
be	called	could	do	good
has	have	he	how	I
into	is	many	more	no
new	of	one	only	other
over	people	should	so	some
their	there	these	they	through
to	two	very	water	was
we	were	what	when	which
who	work	would	you	your

Answers

Chapter 3

1. The three things to check before beginning an ELSA placement test are ... hearing, vision, and medical condition. (page 96)
2. The purpose of the placement test is ... to find out precisely what the pupil can and cannot do. (page 96)
3. The four components of an ELSA teaching objective are ... materials, instructions, pupil performance, and recommended criteria. (pages 96 and 97)
4. The details of the pupil's test performance should be recorded ... in the placement test column of the ELSA records. (pages 97 and 98)
5. The three pieces of information to be recorded for each teaching objective assessed are ... the date, the number of correct responses, and the number of incorrect responses. (pages 97 and 98)
6. The information provided to help you decide which units to assess in a placement test are ... the 'entry skills' which are described on the topsheet of each unit. (page 98)
7. The only guideline provided for deciding which teaching objectives to assess in any unit is ... *all* the objectives in any unit should be assessed. (page 98)

Chapter 4

1. The objectives which you can assume need no further teaching or practice are ... those in which the pupil achieves the recommended criteria in the placement test. (page 102)
2. You may decide to reduce or change the recommended criteria of a teaching objective ... only if a child has a sensory or physical disability which adversely and directly affects his performance on it. (page 103)
3. The teaching objective to be taught first is ... the one on which the pupil is most likely to succeed, i.e. the one in which he was nearest to the recommended criteria on the placement test. (page 102)
4. The guideline for deciding the teaching order of the remaining objectives is ... the same as answer 3, by sequencing the remaining objectives according to the nearness to the recommended criterion during the placement test. (page 102)
5. Certainly more than one objective can be taught simultaneously. (page 102)
6. You should record your decisions about the order of teaching objectives ... on the topsheet of the unit. (page 102)

Chapter 5

1. The three phases of teaching are ... reducing errors, increasing fluency, and applying skills. (page 106)
2. When a pupil begins work on a new objective concentrate on ... improving his accuracy of response. (pages 106 and 107)
3. 'Teaching to errors' involves ... recording the errors made during a placement test and concentrating attention on the failed parts or components of an objective. (pages 106 to 107)
4. During the 'reducing errors' phase the child needs ... a high degree of close supervision and individual attention. (page 107)
5. At the stage of 'increasing fluency' the pupil is ... learning to perform skills more quickly which he can already perform accurately. (page 107)
6. The purpose of the 'applying skills' phase is ... to make sure that the skill described in the teaching objective can be generalized and adopted to other situations. (page 107 to 108)
7. The materials provided in ELSA may be insufficient ... to sustain interest and motivation over an extended period. (page 108)
8. Praise and reward can be used more systematically (and therefore more effectively) with ELSA ... because you are administering praise and reward according to the pupil's measured progress towards the achievement of clearly stated objectives. (pages 109 and 110)
9. With ELSA, parents and classroom helpers can be used ... to consolidate and increase the fluency levels of previously learnt skills. (pages 110 and 111)
10. Children who know their own objectives are more likely to achieve them. (page 110)

Chapter 6

1. If ELSA records are kept up-to-date you will know ... what the child can do, what he is currently working on, and what has yet to be started. (page 114)
2. Previously mastered objectives should be checked ... to ensure that learnt skills are not forgotten. (page 114)
3. The three columns in the ELSA records are ... 'working on', 'mastered', and 'checked'. (page 114)
4. The date should be written in these columns. (page 114)
5. The most relevant assessment information the teacher can have is ... about what the child already knows. (page 114)
6. When using ELSA assessment is ... continuous. (page 114)

0114
2722022